Natyacharya

Sisir Kumar Bhaduri

Pioneer of Modern Indian Theatre

AF668530

Natyacharya

Sisir Kumar Bhaduri

Pioneer of Modern Indian Theatre

Amal Mitra

Compiled and Edited by

Lab Kumar Bose

Foreword by

Samik Bandyopadhyay

Introduction by

Prof. Ananda Lal

NIYOGI
BOOKS

Published by
NIYOGI BOOKS
Block D, Building No. 77,
Okhla Industrial Area, Phase-I,
New Delhi-110 020, INDIA
Tel: 91-11-26816301, 26818960
Email: niyogibooks@gmail.com
Website: www.niyogibooksindia.com

Text © Lab Kumar Bose
Images © Lab Kumar Bose

Editor: Srotoswini Majumdar
Design: Shraboni Roy

ISBN: 978-93-86906-21-2
Publication: 2018

All rights are reserved. No part of this publication may be reproduced or transmitted in any form or by any means, electronic or mechanical, including photocopying, recording or by any information storage and retrieval system without prior written permission and consent of the Publisher.

Printed at: Niyogi Offset Pvt. Ltd., New Delhi, India

Dedicated to my dear wife, Purabi,
and my daughters, Chaitali and Purbali,
who helped in the compilation of the book.

Lab Kumar Bose
Editor

CONTENTS

FOREWORD

I have treasured for long in my personal library Amal Mitra's *Kolkatay Bideshi Rangalay*, and clippings of several articles by him in the daily *Hindusthan Standard*, and also Sisir Kumar Bhaduri's piece published in *Hindusthan Standard*, now included in the present collection, edited by Mr Lab Kumar Bose.

It is a pity that there is no biography in English, documenting the life and work of Sisir Kumar Bhaduri (1889–1959), who, way back in the 1920s, brought modernism to Indian theatre, breaking away from the strongly entrenched 'heroic' histrionics of the decadent British actor-managerial tradition inherited by the Bengali professional theatre that developed in the theatre 'district' in north Kolkata in the 1860s, drawing on the theatre aesthetics that came with the colonial knowledge package. As a conscientious teacher of English literature, Bhaduri followed and responded to the Shaw-Granville Barker-Poel-Gordon Craig upheaval in British theatre at the turn of the century, and focused on psychological realism in stage characterization and mise-en-scene on historical principles when he came to theatre after a short spell of graduate teaching at a Kolkata college. As he explored the psychological prehistory of the characters, and provided them with realistic 'locations' on stage, and developed a pace of performance that allowed his spectators time and leisure to probe, read and brood beyond their stage presence, Bengali theatre had its first taste of realism.

In an interview (published in the periodical *Parichay*), Sombhu Mitra told me in 1965, 'In his early phase, in every production, Sisir Kumar as *prayogkarta* paid attention to every aspect of the production . . . He is perhaps the first full-blown director in our theatre who had a vision of total theatre. We could not have started our work if he had not been there. He created total theatre in Bengal, and that alone enables us to raise theatre to a level of deeper sensitivity. We couldn't have made the move without him . . . His acting was not a matter of a string of memorable pieces of performance. Watching him act, I had felt for the first time that here was a man with whom every word he spoke and every gesture he made was loaded with meaning. He got the meaning into his acting.'

With all the passionate commitment that a band of young intellectuals led by Hemendrakumar Roy, Manilal Gangopadhyay, Sunitikumar Chatterjee, Rakhaldas Banerjee and Abanindranath Taogre brought to their valorization of Sisir Kumar's achievements and originality—particularly in the pages of *Nautchghar*, a theatre periodical they brought out—they could not create the perceptive audience that Bhaduri needed to carry his breakthrough forward. The theatre culture that could recognize the new values inherent in Bhaduri's creativity came into being in Bengal only in the 1960s, through a long and slow process of orientation that began with the IPTA in the 1940s, and matured in the exposure to and appreciation of the works of Bijan Bhattacharya, Sombhu Mitra, Utpal Dutt and Ajitesh Bandyopadhyay.

Bhaduri's US tour was a financial disaster that left him a wreck on his return. It affected his theatre, his creative freedom alike, and he was literally thrown out of his theatre and his private flat in the same building by the landlord in 1956 as a defaulter on the rent. The last three years of his life he had no theatre, no theatre company to call his own. But the mind and the imagination remained as alert as ever, as we found for ourselves when we gathered around him twice a week in 1958 to listen to him and read the plays that he had once directed and performed, with productional / performative details that he shared with us so generously. But the pain of the US debacle endured. On 2 October 1958, as we celebrated his last birthday with him, at one point, he said with seething bitterness, 'No foreigner will ever be a friend of mine!'

Even as I cherish my memories of those few rare evenings with the Master and the last few performances he put up with members of his old company, by then folded up, on special occasions and for a short retrospective in December 1958 (I watched him in *Reetimato Natak*), his last stage appearance, less than a month before his death on 30 May 1959), I consider myself privileged, and share the sentiments that Sombhu Mitra added to my transcript of his interview with me, in his own handwriting: 'For us who have gained from our viewing of those theatrical masterpieces by Sisir Kumar, our reference for theatre will perhaps be different. That is what keeps us indebted to him.'

I would still hope that someone someday will write a biography of Sisir Kumar Bhaduri in English, something to match the thoroughly researched and documented biography in Bengali by Shankar Bhattacharya. But so long as such a biography is not there, Amal Mitra's short essays will be of great value to readers, scholars and theatre practitioners looking for an entry point to the history of modern Indian theatre, and the history of the emergence of the *prayogkarta* (incidentally, it was a coinage by Tagore that he used to describe Sisir Kumar), the modern director, no longer a *nirdeshak* (lit. manager-controller)—but a creative maker / master.

Samik Bandyopadhyay

PREFACE

The eminent and gifted actor of the modern Bengali stage, Sisir Kumar Bhaduri (1889–1959), brought a new era in Bengali theatre.

A keen student of English and ancient Greek literature, Sisir Kumar Bhaduri earned a Master's degree in English from Presidency College under the University of Calcutta and then became a very popular professor of English at Metropolitan College (presently Vidyasagar College), Calcutta. He also took a keen amateur interest in Bengali theatre and regularly participated in various plays. He produced and directed Dwijendra Lal Roy's *Chandragupta* in 1914, enacted by undergraduate and postgraduate students of the university (a leaflet of the production is included in the Annexure).

Quite against the norm of the times, he quit his academic career and joined professional theatre in 1921, participating in over eighty productions afterwards. He made his mark not merely as an actor of unmatched genius, but also as a pioneering director. He made radical changes in scenography, costumes, lighting, music and choreography. His work was acknowledged and praised even in the western world. In 1930, he and his troupe were invited to the United States to perform on the New York stage, where he was given a Mayor's Reception. On his return to India, he was given the privilege of a Command Performance by the Viceroy of India.

Amal Mitra, the well-known literary personality, was acquainted with renowned writers, artists and famous personalities of the Bengali stage over a long period and thus had an in-depth knowledge of twentieth-century Bengali literature and life. His series of articles on the English theatre in Calcutta, published in the prestigious Bengali magazine *Dainik Basumati*, received much appreciation from Sisir Kumar Bhaduri and they later became close friends.

Amal Mitra's research work on Calcutta's English stage was published as a book in 1967—*Kolkatay Bideshi Rangalay*. It was highly acclaimed by critics, academicians and historians and is prescribed as a reference book for the Master of Arts course in Bengali at both the Calcutta and Rabindra Bharati Universities. His excellent article on Rabindranath Tagore and Sisir Kumar prompted the Tagore Research Institute to publish his book titled *Kabiguru Rabindranath and Nataraj Sisir Kumar* in 1977.

I myself had the rare privilege of watching many of Sisir Kumar's plays, such as *Sita*, *Takht-e-Taus*, *Alamgir*, *Ritimato Natak*, *Michael Madhusudan*, *Bijaya*, *Parichay*, *Chandragupta*, *Rama* and *Palli Samaj* during my college days. His performances were resoundingly impressive and fascinating. I was also blessed with the rare opportunity of being party to his 61st birthday celebration on 2 October 1950, organized by noted historian Dr Kalidas Nag along with Dadathakur (Sarat Chandra Pandit) and Amal Mitra. Sisir Kumar had discussed at length various aspects of the Bengali theatre. He expressed his view that 'a nation is known by its stage' and wanted the Government to build a separate academy for educating children on drama and theatre.

Amal Mitra wrote various articles on Sisir Kumar, published in journals and newspapers. They give details about his life, his interactions and his meetings with famous personalities like Girish Chandra Ghosh, Rabindranath Tagore and Sarat Chandra Chatterjee. They cover many aspects of his role as a director and art designer with a detailed eye for scenic backdrops and costumes ensuring a grand experience for audiences. Sisir Kumar had taken Bengali theatre to world-class levels. The article 'Sisir Kumar Bhaduri in the Eyes of Foreigners' highlights how his plays had touched the hearts of English,

European, Russian and American spectators and had received great acclaim from all. In his writings, Amal Mitra received suggestions and guidance from Dr Suniti Kumar Chatterjee, Dr Kalidas Nag, Hemendra Kumar Ghose, Hemendra Kumar Roy, Parimal Goswami and Ashoke Bhaduri (Sisir Kumar's son).

This book is a compilation of the original English essays by Amal Mitra on Sisir Kumar, along with other interesting material. I had been in possession of them because Amal Mitra was my uncle. A famous article by Sisir Kumar himself after declining the honour of Padma Bhushan bestowed by the Government of India, and seeking the establishment of a National Theatre in Calcutta, has been incorporated. A number of unpublished photographs of Sisir Kumar have also been included. I hope that this book will reinvigorate interest in the great contribution of Sisir Kumar to modern Bengali theatre, and will help students, researchers and teachers as well as those interested in the evolution of Bengali theatre.

I am thankful to Professor Ananda Lal, the noted theatre scholar, for taking the initiative to facilitate publication of this book and agreeing to write the introduction. I am grateful to Sri Nirmal Bhattacharjee of Niyogi Books for agreeing to publish the book. I also express my thanks to all those who helped in its compilation.

Lab Kumar Bose, *Editor*

**Lab Kumar Bose, former Executive Director, Coal India Ltd, a nephew of Amal Mitra, was associated with his uncle's publications since his student days. He was responsible for editing various proceedings of the Mining, Geological and Metallurgical Institute of India, including those of the 1st (2006), 2nd (2008), 3rd (2010), 5th (2014) and 6th (2016) Asian Mining Congresses, and also the World Mining Congress (2003).

INTRODUCTION

Public knowledge about Indian theatre history is sadly deficient, caused by a systemic failure to sensitize and educate people about our arts in general, as well as the prevalent misconception that theatre in our country matured and became modern only after Independence. Consequently, if the lay reader knows anything at all about the pioneers and pillars of the Indian stage, these are likely to be post-1947 personalities such as Sombhu Mitra, Habib Tanvir, Ebrahim Alkazi et al. The fact that nineteenth and early twentieth-century giants like Bharatendu Harishchandra, Girish Chandra Ghosh or B. P. Kirloskar shaped modern theatre in their respective languages, and how they did so, remains neglected, especially in international, national or non-regional mediums like English. The contribution of Sisir Kumar Bhaduri falls under this eclipse, his work 'as the first director proper in modern Indian theatre'[1] largely unknown. No book exists in English devoted to his career and achievements.[2] This one, therefore, marks a significant breakthrough.

I shall very briefly define here the main reasons for bestowing that prestigious laurel on Sisir Kumar Bhaduri. First, as a student and then college teacher of English in Calcutta during the second decade of the century, he kept abreast of the latest trends on the British stage, importing them into Bengali theatre and thereby continuing its development from the 1920s onward. This statement requires some explanation. One could argue that awareness of foreign theatre was nothing special at that time, given that most of Indian theatre drew heavily from its visual grandeur and latest technology. But we must differentiate between that populist and commercial phenomenon, and Bhaduri's more academic and 'serious' explorations. The theory and practice of modernistic realism had been established by Ibsen and Stanislavsky in European 'little theatres' or art theatres by 1900; but it had not been accepted by the Indian stage at all, which preferred the older melodramatic style that clicked at the box office. Professional Indian producers had no use for restrained and non-musical social realism, nor did they think that in-depth study and research had any place in public entertainment.

Bhaduri changed that approach. Consciously attempting to reform the commercial Bengali stage, he incorporated the new techniques in his productions. He began to ignore the standard Victorian lush mise-en-scene framed by wings at the sides, and encouraged artists like Charu Roy to design box sets and zonal lighting. He directed his actors in psychological naturalism, away from the conventional extravagance and rhetorical flourish. These innovations drew a different section of Calcutta's population into playhouses: the intellectuals and those of refined taste, who had abjured the 'cheap' theatrics of Bhaduri's precursors but appreciated his changes and campaigned for him in their own writings. The most illustrious example proving this transformation lies in the conversion of Rabindranath Tagore. He gave Bhaduri exclusive permission to stage his revolutionary masterpiece *Raktakaravi* (*Red Oleander*), even before it was published, and the production was eagerly anticipated by the press in 1924–25 but, unfortunately, it never materialized.[3]

Nonetheless, Tagore's close theatrical relationship with Bhaduri continued, and Amal Mitra devotes a full chapter to it. Allow me to quote in short from my own book on Tagore:

> 'Tagore generally avoided contact with the Bengali professional stage because it really had nothing to offer him; its dependence on

> commercial success precluded any attempts at experimentation, and Tagore justifiably had no wish to compromise his dramatic principles. …[However, he] held Bhaduri's talents as director and actor in special regard, and at the latter's request he revised one of his earlier farces, renaming it *Sesh Raksha*, for performance by Natyamandir. Bhaduri's production on 7 September 1927 was a spectacular event, notable historically for the first use of audience participation on the Bengali stage: Bhaduri broke the proscenium barrier between stage and auditorium, and in the final scene invited the spectators to join the wedding festivities in the play. The house responded with great enthusiasm, singing along with the marriage songs and intermingling with the cast on stage in celebration of the happy ending. Inspired by this smash success Bhaduri tried his hand at a complex Tagore play, *Tapati*, staging it on 25 December 1929.'[4]

Besides this understanding of cutting-edge original drama, Bhaduri shared with his great predecessor, Girish Ghosh, a quality that set them apart from most of the rest of their tribe. Furthermore, given the conditions of Bengali theatre today, one can observe that this important trait in the two of them is sorely lacking in the majority of present Bengali directors. Because of their open mind to theatre from all over the world, Ghosh and Bhaduri, particularly the latter, used to regularly frequent performances by visiting foreign companies in Calcutta. For a theatre artist, it is imperative to know the international state of the art from first-hand experience rather than simply literature or hearsay. I do not find this desire as evident as it should be in contemporary Bengali directors and theatre workers, as a result of which the movement has grown progressively insular and even dated, alienating younger viewers too. Bhaduri demonstrated a much more liberal attitude, which was indeed needed, and that amounted to what we call cosmopolitanism nowadays.

An interesting intercultural encounter, though ultimately not very positive, occurred in Bhaduri's career that deserves attention here before the reader goes on to Amal Mitra's account of it in this book. A British actor, Eric Elliott, had come to Calcutta and seen Bhaduri's production of *Sita*.[5] He was impressed enough to want Bhaduri's company to perform in the West. With the active help of Satu Sen, a Bengali student who had become assistant director-manager of the famous American Laboratory Theatre in New York and later joined the National School of Drama in New Delhi as its first Director, Elliott managed to organize funds for Natyamandir's trip to New York in 1930. Bhaduri led seven performances of *Sita* at the Vanderbilt Theatre on Broadway in January 1931. The unfamiliar play and style received mixed reviews, the praise no doubt influenced by the exotica of the content. Mitra reprinted the opinions of one critic comparing Bhaduri very favourably with the legendary Chinese actor Mei Lanfang, who had performed in New York the previous year. I excerpt below a representative paragraph that Mitra excluded from another review that he extracted:

'The acting differed sometimes from the Western Style, and so did the overhead lighting and the music—yet it was all effective. If theatre-goers desire to see a drama that will take them far away from Broadway, here is their opportunity.' [6]

Historically, Bhaduri's venture was important as possibly the earliest instance of an Indian production touring the USA. Before that, only one Parsi company from Bombay, the Victoria Theatrical Company, is known to have played in London, at the colonial exhibition in 1885. Mitra tells us that Bhaduri even received an invitation to go to the USSR following good reports from Russians who viewed his acting in Calcutta, but he was unable to take up the offer.

In the year of Bhaduri's death, 1959, the Government of India announced the award of the nation's third-highest civilian decoration, the Padma Bhushan, to him. Most Indians would be proud to accept such an honour, but Bhaduri declined it. This action shows his courage to stand up for what he believed. He refused the award because the country had not given its people a national theatre, which Bhaduri had espoused strongly. His argument during the 1950s for such an institution has become the stuff of legend in theatrical circles, but few Indians have access to the text today. The editor of the present book has most helpfully provided in an appendix Bhaduri's response in the form of an article to question about the national theatre, which will help scholars and researchers.

A final word about the impeccable credentials of the author: Amal Mitra's scholarship on theatre is recognized in Bengali, but his popular writings in English based on the material he collected are less well known.[7] Thanks to the editor, Lab Kumar Bose, Mitra's articles on Bhaduri, printed in Calcutta's now defunct English daily *The Hindustan Standard*, have been preserved and made available at last. Otherwise they would have suffered the fate of so much valuable, uncatalogued, periodical literature in India—lost like the proverbial needles in a haystack in our musty, disorganized libraries and archives or, worse, so brittle that they disintegrate irretrievably.

Ananda Lal, *Professor*
Jadavpur University, Kolkata

Endnotes

1 Swapan Majumdar, *"Bhaduri, Sisir Kumar"*, in Ananda Lal, ed., The Oxford Companion to Indian Theatre (New Delhi: Oxford University Press, 2004), 46.

2. Among chapters in the few English books on Bengali theatre, the one on Bhaduri by Kironmoy Raha in *Bengali Theatre* (New Delhi: National Book Trust, 1993), 102-126, is the most informative. The award-winning Bengali author Sunil Gangopadhyay also wrote a novel on Bhaduri available in English as "The Lonely Emperor", in *Classic Sunil Gangopadhyay*, translated by Aruna Chakravarti and Sreejata Guha (New Delhi: Penguin, 2013).

3. Rabindranath Tagore, *Three Plays*, translated and with an introduction by Ananda Lal, 2nd ed. (New Delhi: Oxford University Press, 2001), 130.

4. Tagore, *Three Plays*, trans. Lal, 38-39.

5. Sushil Kumar Mukherjee, *The Story of the Calcutta Theatres: 1753-1980* (Calcutta: K. P. Bagchi, 1982), 199-200. An actor by the name of Eric Elliott did perform occasionally in London during the 1920s. However, Mitra says Elliott was a Flight Lieutenant in the Royal Air Force.

6. Stephen Rathburn, *"Oriental Classic"*, New York Sun, 13 January 1931. Quoted in Mukherjee, 201-2. But see Mukherjee, 202-3, for two highly negative reviews that appeared in the New York Times and The World.

7. For another collection, see Amal Mitra, *English Stage in India: 18th & 19th Century*, ed. Lab Kumar Bose (Kolkata: Dasgupta & Co., 2012).

Letter from Sri Sisir Kumar Bhaduri,*
"The great master of Indian drama of the 20th Century"

SRIRANGAM
2A, RAJA RAJKISSEN STREET

Phone : B.B. 556 Calcutta, Sunday, 5th April '53

Dear Sri Amal Mitra,

I have been studying your articles on development of English Stage in Calcutta as published in Basumati every week. I appreciate them very much. There is great relevance on such research work. I shall feel very happy if these articles are published in a book.

With blessings to you,

Yours Sincerely,
Sisir Kumar Bhaduri

* Translated from original letter in Bengali.

NATYACHARYA

SISIR KUMAR BHADURI

(1889–1959)

NATYACHARYA SISIR KUMAR BHADURI (1889-1959)

In view of the 73rd Birthday Anniversary of Natyacharya Sisir Kumar Bhaduri which was observed at a public meeting at the University Institute Hall, Calcutta, on October 2, the following article, we hope, will be read with interest.

—Editor, *The Sunday Hindusthan Standard.*

The 19th century was unquestionably one of the most glorious periods in the history of Bengal; numerous people of outstanding genius were born in that century and their distinguished labours in the varied spheres of religion, education, social reform, literature, science and the dramatic art lent great lustre to the country's reputation. That pre-eminent and gifted actor of the modern Bengali stage who brought in a new era in the theatre of Bengal, Sisir Kumar Bhaduri, was also born in that century (2nd October 1889) in the Midnapore house of his maternal grandfather Krishna Kishore Acharya. It might be appropriate to recount here some of the achievements of Krishna Kishore, as he exercised considerable influence on the formation of the grandson's character. It was from Krishna Kishore that Sisir Kumar Bhaduri acquired to a large extent his thirst for knowledge and his love of literature. Krishna Kishore was Secretary of the Midnapore District Board and one of the most popular and highly respected residents of Midnapore.

Very well versed in the literature and history of Bengal, the scholarly Krishna Kishore would regularly contribute articles of great distinction to the paper *Medini Bandhab*. Sisir Kumar Bhaduri spent a great deal of his time in his grandfather's library, which had a small but remarkably well-selected collection of books. Under his grandfather's guidance, Sisir Kumar Bhaduri studied at an early age such subjects as English literature and ancient Greek literature etc. He would frequently refer in later life the great contribution in his teaching career that his grandfather's instruction had made for him.

The Bhaduris were descended from the well-known Subudhdhi Khan Bhaduri, and their ancestral home was in the district of Rajshahi, Sisir Kumar Bhaduri's paternal great grandfather, Jaygopal Khan Bhaduri, settled in Santragachi near Calcutta. Sisir Kumar Bhaduri's father, Haridas Bhaduri, after qualifying at the Roorkee Engineering College, joined the P.W.D. as a supervisor; his exceptional knowledge and skill earned him promotion to the post of Assistant Executive Engineer. A man of independent mind and strong principles, he did not hesitate to resign from government service when a certain measure on the part of his superiors struck him as unjust. Sisir Kumar Bhaduri inherited from his father these qualities of independence of mind and self-respect. Sisir Kumar Bhaduri's mother Kamalekamini Devi was a lady of high ideals and outstanding qualities who played a very important part in the development of her son's character, acting as his guide, philosopher and friend, and inspired the very greatest devotion in Sisir Kumar Bhaduri.

Sisir Kumar Bhaduri's formal education started when he was quite young. Later he was admitted to the Bangabashi School and passed the entrance examination at the remarkably early age of 14. He then took his degree from the G. A. Institution (now the Scottish

Church College) and went on to Presidency College, from which he took his Master's degree in English in the year 1913. A great deal has been recounted about his student career by his intimate friends Dr Suniti Kumar Chatterjee, Dr Srikumar Banerjee and others, and no detailed account is therefore required in this article.

It should be mentioned, however, that as an exceptionally meritorious student he was most popular with all his teachers such as Barada Sanyal at school and Prof. James at college; they naturally hoped for great things from him. It might be remarked that Prof. James could often be observed peering into the college library to see if his favourite student were there, absorbed in a study of literature or drama when he should have been in class. Any time Sisir Kumar Bhaduri was so discovered he was naturally packed off to the classroom at once. Sisir Kumar Bhaduri also joined the Law College and was articled to that well-known lawyer Dasarathi Sanyal. His father was anxious that Sisir Kumar Bhaduri should take up a legal career, but this line never appealed to him.

Instead, he took up the post of a Professor at the Metropolitan (now Vidyasagar) College as soon as he had acquired his Master's degree. In later life Sisir Kumar Bhaduri would recount an amusing story in this connection. Being very young for Professors he and his friend Prof. Pannalal Mukherjee decided to take to smoking cigars so as to create an impression of dignity and gravity in the minds of the students. Whether or not he succeeded in his purpose, he would say he could never thereafter break himself of the habit of smoking cigars.

Actually he was extremely popular with his students as many of his ex students will unhesitatingly confirm even today. As a handsome and youthful professor he combined with a profound knowledge of English literature, drama and poetry in particular, a most mellifluous speaking voice and his delivery was excellent. Students were most reluctant to miss his lectures. His fame spread far and wide and it was not unusual for students of other colleges to come in to hear him speak; unfortunately, his independence of mind caused him to come into friction with the college authorities on certain important issues and he tendered his resignation in January 1921. He was relieved of his duties on the first of February that year. This proved a blessing in disguise for the future of the Bengali stage.

It was in the same month that Sisir Kumar Bhaduri tendered his resignation of the post of Professor that Madan, hearing from Rai Bahadur P.N. Mukherjee, of his exceptional ability as an amateur actor, asked him to join his newly established Bengali Theatrical Co. The social conventions of the day were highly conservative and most unprogressive; it was unheard of for a professor to take up a career on the professional stage. It was with considerable hesitation and uncertainty, therefore, that Sisir Kumar Bhaduri entered his new career, for which he first sought the permission and blessings of his mother. He was plagued with considerable pecuniary difficulties at that time.

Since his father's death in 1915 he had to support the entire family of numerous members. Tragedy struck too at that time in the death (1916) of his wife, Usha Devi, the daughter of Agra's renowned medical practitioner Rai Bahadur Dr Nabin Ch. Chakravarty. One son had been born to them.

There had been indications even during his college days of the great dramatic skill possessed by the individual who was destined to rise to the top of the professional stage in Bengal. Indeed there were suggestions of it even when he was at school. He would compete in the recitation contests held at school. On one occasion, in order to make certain that there should be no defect in his delivery of a recitation at one of these competitions, Charu Ch. Gupta, the son of Mahendranath Gupta, a disciple of Sri Ramakrishna, took him along to the greatest actor of the Bengali stage at that time, Girish Chandra Ghosh. The eminent actor was enthralled with young Sisir Kumar Bhaduri's excellent recitation of a portion of *Meghnadbadh Kavya*. He corrected him in just one or two places and then said – '*My boy, you will do very well, your tone of voice is excellent and your delivery most impressive and fascinating.*' Needless to say, Sisir Kumar Bhaduri won the competition without any difficulty.

In performances of *Julius Caesar* at the Scottish Church College and of *Hamlet*, *Kurukshetra*, *Jana*, *Ashoka*, *Raghubir* etc. at the Calcutta University Institute (C.U.I.), Sisir Kumar Bhaduri demonstrated his genius as an actor. His most impressive performance at the C.U.I. was in the role of Chanakya in the play *Chandragupta* (18th Sept 1911). The play was so well performed that the dramatist himself and others such as Sir Gurudas Banerjee, Sir Asutosh Mukherjee, Prof. Manmatha Mohon Bose, Prof. Benoyendra Nath Sen etc. were most favourably impressed. They lavished particular praise on Sisir Kumar Bhaduri's performance. Another performance put on at that time is worthy of mention. This was the performance of Rabindranath's *Baikunther Khata,* attended by Gurudev himself at a special show put on by the members in honour of his 50th birthday. Rabindranath was delighted with the performance. In a letter (23rd Magh 1318 BS) to Amal Home he expressed the opinion that so skilful a rendering of this play could not have been achieved by anyone at all, save only those members of the Tagore family itself, Gaganendranath and Abanindranath. He added – 'I envied the one playing the role of Kedar. Once I attained fame in this role myself.'

It was, of course, Sisir Kumar Bhaduri who had played the role of Kedar. This was in 1911, when Sisir Kumar Bhaduri was still a student. The poet's prophetic eye unhesitatingly fastened on the talent for acting that the future stage celebrity possessed. This was the first occasion on which the poet had seen Sisir Kumar Bhaduri perform on the stage, the actor later became a great favourite of Rabindranath, who was so enthralled with his acting skill that he described him as the *Nataraj* of the Bengali stage. So confident was the poet of Sisir Kumar Bhaduri's ability to put on a good stage performance that he unhesitatingly allowed him to stage a number of his plays such as *Bisarjan*, *Tapati*, *Sesh-raksha* etc. He also came to see Sisir Kumar Bhaduri in numerous other stage performances such as *Sita*, *Ritimata Natak* etc. and was most lavish in his praise of his acting and directing abilities.

As a member of the C.U. Institute Sisir Kumar Bhaduri was most active. For many years he was the Under Secretary of the Institute (1909–1913). Dr Srikumar Banerjee's statement quoted below will give a good idea of the very great popularity that Sisir Kumar Bhaduri enjoyed among the members and others associated with the Institute on account of his outstanding personality his charm and culture, and his deep erudition in literature and poetry. It will also serve to emphasize the great influence he exerted on the members. Dr Banerjee says –

> 'There was among them, Sisir Bhaduri, with his fine Apollo-like presence with his quick and keen enjoyment of poetry, his flair for recitation, and his wonderful histrionic talents already pregnant with the promise of a great future. With brilliant conversational powers ready of wit and quick in repartee, daringly unconventional in his thoughts and ways of life, a dissenter by temperament titling at the established goods of our worship, he cast a spell which few could escape and drew round him a crowd of devoted followers… There were keen discussions on controversial topics… one of the frequent subjects on which we argued was the poetry of Rabindranath

> which was at the time just coming into its own and emerging from the mists of misunderstanding and prejudice. Here again, Sisir Bhaduri was champion of novelty against the conservative advocacy of the older poets like Hem Chandra and Nabin Chandra. He did a lot of service in the introducing to many of us the poems of Rabindranath, specially the stirring, musical narrations of *Katha-O-Kahini*. In these controversies his fine powers of recitation won half the battle for him, achieving quicker results than the creeping, slow-paced process of argument could have compassed.' (C.U.I. Diamond Jubilee Souvenir).

At that time too his superb qualities as an actor greatly impressed the members of the audiences in performances staged by the Old Club.

To revert to Sisir Kumar Bhaduri's connection with the Bengali Theatrical Co. it may be remarked that starting his professional career with *Alamgir* (10th Oct. 1921) he was with the above-mentioned Company for a period of about a year and a half. Disagreeing with the management in various important points connected with their stage presentations, Sisir Kumar Bhaduri left the company. After that he assembled his own troupe and put on a performance of D.L. Roy's *Sita* on the stage in the Eden Gardens Exhibition (1923). Later he started his own theatre at the premises of the Alfred play house on 8th Chaitra 1330 BS.

The new era that Sisir Kumar Bhaduri was to introduce in the Bengali stage, however, may be said to date from the time he staged Jogesh Ch. Chowdhuri's *Sita* at the Monmohon Theatre. It may be mentioned here that to start his theatre on the Monmohon stage he had to incur a debt of about seventy-five thousand rupees at a very high rate of interest. On the opening night (6th Aug. 1924) the inaugural ceremony was performed by that celebrated actor and playwright Amritalal Bose in the presence of a most distinguished audience including Deshbandhu C.R. Das and such other celebrities. In his neat little speech Amritalal Bose declared that now that Sisir Kumar Bhaduri had appeared, the degraded Bengali stage would be rehabilitated by him, and so he, an old man, could die in peace.

The performance of *Sita* was a tremendous success. To quote Sourendranath Mukherjee –

> 'Sita ran for over a year and a half without break playing to packed houses. There were no jubilee celebrations in those days......it was not customary to have an elaborate celebration if a play managed to run for a hundred nights. *Sita* ran for all that time purely on its own merits.'

It was at this theatre that the audiences of those days were privileged to see outstanding performances of plays such as *Pasani*, *Jana*, *Bhisma*, *Raghubir* etc. The building was subsequently acquired by the Improvement Trust and Sisir Kumar Bhaduri moved to what is now the Sree Cinema (1926). At this theatre too his outstanding performances in plays such as *Bisarjan*, *Tapati*, *Sesh-raksha*, *Digbijoyee*, *Sorosi*, *Pratapaditya*, *Prafulla*, *Bilwamangal*, *Sadhabar Ekadashi*, *Balidan*, *Bhramar*, *Buddhadev* and *Sankhya Dhyani* etc, would enthrall and fascinate members of the audience both Indian and foreign, night after night.

In 1930 Sisir Kumar Bhaduri proceeded to America to appear on the New York stage. He scored an outstanding success there and returned to India in the following year. It was in that year that he appeared in a command performance of *Sita* in New Delhi, attended by the Viceroy and many other dignitaries. What a very favourable impression the performance made on the Viceroy and his wife will be abundantly clear from a letter (March 21 1931) that the Military Secretary of the Viceroy wrote to Bhaduri. He said in this letter –

> 'The fact that we were able to follow the play although we could not understand a word of the language in itself says much for the acting. Their Excellencies were quite thrilled with it and desire me to offer you their warm congratulations.'

It was in 1931 too that Sisir Kumar Bhaduri appeared again on the Calcutta stage in a performance of *Sri Sri Bishnupriya* put on at the Rangmahal stage. Thereafter he directed Natyaniketan for a while and then set up his own theatre at the premises of the Star (28th July 1934). A great many people today must remember with the keenest enjoyment his excellent acting in plays staged at this theatre such as *Bijoya*, *Ritimata Natak*, *Jogajog* etc.

For a number of reasons he gave up the Star Theatre premises and set up another theatre of his own named Srirangam at the premises of the old Natyaniketan in the year 1942. At this new theatre he staged a number of successful performances of plays such as *Jivan Ranga*, *Urochiti*, *Deshbandhu*, *Parichaya*, *Michael Madhusudan*, *Takht-e-taus* etc. Unfortunately, however, he was not able to keep this theatre going and it closed down in January 1956.

Thereafter he only appeared occasionally on the stage but it was evident from his performances that in spite of his age he had lost none of his acting skill. The outstanding successes achieved as an actor and producer by the imitator of the modern Bengali stage during his long career can best be summed up by stating without fear of contradiction that there is not a single actor today who could match his performances in the various roles he played. It may be mentioned here that he appeared on the stage in about eighty different roles.

It may be mentioned here that he also appeared in and directed a number of screen performances. Films of the stories of that great writer Sarat Chandra Chatterjee are very popular today. It was

Sisir Kumar Bhaduri who produced the first film version of a story (*Andhare Alo*) of Sarat Chandra.

It is unfortunate that many of the aspirations of this shaper of the modern Bengali stage remained unfulfilled when he died (30th June 1959). He wanted to stage a Festival of Drama to celebrate the Centenary of the Bengali drama, but this could not be done. Another ambition he cherished was to set up a National theatre. Before independence it was Deshbandhu C.R. Das who supported him in this venture, and promised to collect all the money necessary for that. His sudden death, however, rendered the scheme abortive. After Independence the West Bengal Government offered Sisir Kumar Bhaduri financial assistance before the Srirangam was finally closed. Financially embarrassed as he was at the time, he nevertheless stuck to his firm principles and finding himself at variance with the Government on numerous points he declined the offer.

He accepted the parliamentary address of West Bengal Congress in 1955 because he said that Congress were the rulers of the country and that this recognition accorded to him amounted to State recognition of the theatre.

His principles compelled him to refuse the title of Padma Bhushan offered to him by the Government in the year 1959. He desired no title in recognition of his life-long dedication to the stage. What he desired from the Government was the establishment of a National Theatre for the benefit of the people which, in his words, should be 'a truly National theatre and not a nationalised theatre.'

First published in *The Sunday Hindustan Standard*, 18.10.1961

SISIR KUMAR BHADURI
A MASTER PRODUCER

SISIR KUMAR BHADURI
A MASTER PRODUCER

A great deal depends upon the producer in the staging of a well-balanced and successful dramatic performance. Quite apart from the acting itself, the costumers, scenery and lighting all demand his careful attention. A certain dramatic critic was therefore entirely right when he expressed the following opinion –

> 'It may seem to the ordinary audience that the presentation of a play depends on the author and the players. But in fact they have comparatively much less to do with mounting the play on the board satisfactorily.
>
> Good author and artistes are of course indispensable for a good production but unless they are piloted by a talented producer, results become far from satisfactory. The producer, in a word, is the man.'

The importance of a producer in all stage shows has long been recognized in the West. Many years elapsed, however, after the Bengali professional stage came into being in 1872 before anyone here began to appreciate the substantial contribution a producer might make to a successful stage performance. One come across the names of a great many actors, playwrights, dramatic instructors and even of managers and proprietors of theatres, but in not a single instance do the old records relating to the Bengali stage make any mention of a producer. There can be little doubt therefore that Sisir Kumar Bhaduri, originator of the new age in the Bengali theatre, was the first and most important stage producer that Bengal has ever had. It would not be inappropriate to mention in this connection that Sisir Kumar Bhaduri undertook the production of stage plays long before he became a professional actor himself. In the year 1914 the members of the Calcutta University Institute staged a play in aid of war funds at the recently demolished premises of the Dalhousie Institute. *Chandragupta,* Annexure-I depicting the cover page of the programme of *Chandragupta,* was the play chosen and a great many distinguished persons such as Pandit Motilal Nehru etc., were present at the performance. Sisir Kumar Bhaduri's name appears on the programme as the producer of this highly successful stage performance which was widely praised.

It was in the twenties of this century that Sisir Kumar Bhaduri first made his mark in stage circle in Calcutta, not merely as an actor of unrivalled genius, but also as a highly talented and competent producer. This was just about the time that the professional stage in Bengal made radical departures from tradition not merely in the mode of acting but also in respect of stage scenery, costumes, stage lighting, music, dances, etc. for much of which that outstanding stage personality Sisir Kumar Bhaduri was responsible. He gathered about him a number of highly talented people whose cooperation helped him to revolutionize the stage in Bengal. It would be no exaggeration to say that it was Sisir Kumar Bhaduri who revived our moribund theatre and infused in it a new lease of life with the innovations he introduced. He had an unfailing gift for picking just the right people for each particular task. It was at his suggestion and under his direction that famous artists such as Jamini Roy, Charu Roy, Ramendranath

Chatterjee, Johur, etc., devoted themselves to the task of painting stage scenery and their magic touch completely transformed the previously drab backgrounds. Flat scenes were replaced by those giving a three-dimensional effect. Lighting effects were likewise radically altered. One of Sisir Kumar Bhaduri's first innovations as producer was to replace footlights as the means of illuminating the stage by lights directed from above or from the wings. The noted musician Gurudas Chatterjee and others helped to bring about a thorough change in the realm of stage music. Dances included in stage performances were set to a new pattern by that great authority on Indian dances Monilal Ganguli and Hemendra Kumar Roy, who is also eminent in this sphere. However much others might have contributed in this way in their respective fields to better stage performances, Sisir Kumar Bhaduri kept a sharp eye on every facet of each play he produced.

It is impossible to describe in a short article the meticulous care that Sisir Kumar Bhaduri took in regard to every single constituent part of a stage performance—music, dancing, scenery etc., to ensure that the play, historical, mythological or of any other variety, should be adequately, appropriately and faithfully presented. I shall therefore concentrate on one particular aspect—that of stage costumes, and attempt to show how skilled a producer he was by indicating the infinite pains he devoted to the selection of the most suitable costumes, in securing which money was no consideration with him.

Before Sisir Kumar Bhaduri's time the Bengali stage had known a great many outstanding actors such as Girish Chandra, Ardhendu Shekhar, etc. Their histrionic skill had held audiences spellbound night after night. It seems, however, that these distinguished artistes thought it sufficient to concentrate on the acting alone and failed to realize the importance of such ancillary aids to a realistic performance as costumes appropriate to the period of any character they happened to represent. In fact so little attention was paid to the selection of suitable costumes that the principal characters in a play would often appear on the stage garbed in such a manner as must have seemed ridiculous to discriminating members of the audience. There was little to distinguish the costume of a Hindu rajah from that of a Muslim nawab. In most cases the costumes would be of velvet or silk elaborately decorated with sparkling jari. Actresses too would often be inappropriately attired. For example, one taking the part of a Mughal empress would sometimes appear in a modern English type of jacket with a typically Muslim ghaghra. The well-known dramatic critic Hemendra Kumar Roy has remarked –

> 'The costumes worn by stage Akbars, Jehangirs, Shajehans, Aurangzebs and other Badshahs, the thrones on which they sit and the articles they handle would seem unbelievable even in a nightmare…I myself have seen an actress playing the part of Nur Jehan come on to the stage dressed in a jacket of typically English design. ……. If the same type of costumes were worn by Girish Chandra playing the role of Raja Lakshman Sen's priest Pasupati at the time of Bukhtiar Khiljee and Dani Babu in the role of the 18th century Nawab Sirajudaulla, the producers of those days seemed to think nothing of it.' (*Bangla Rangalaya O Sisir Kumar*).

This will show what scant attention was paid to costumes in those days.

Sisir Kumar Bhaduri, however, as a producer, was most particular about costumes and made it a special point to see that every single character in a play was clothed in a manner appropriate to its period and station. An intimate friend of his, Dr Suniti Kumar Chatterjee, writing about him, has made it abundantly clear how very particular he was about costumes, even in his early days, before joining the professional stage, when, still a student, he would take part in plays at the college or those staged by the Calcutta University Institute. Dr Chatterjee says –

> '...... That year he set about staging *Julius Caesar*. He was to have appeared in the role of Brutus. The organizers had relied upon costumes to be obtained from an English theatre which was at that time running in the city. Only three or four days were left for the show .They learnt to their dismay that the costumes would not be available. The play could not be abandoned because the prestige of a section of students was at stake. In that quandary, I, with my interest in the picturesque side of history, with two fellow students ventured to prepare proper costumes for the play, using silk chaddars, unsewn pieces of cloth, achkan-like tunics and sandals purchased from the local market. We could produce passable imitations of Roman civil dress. Then we took up the question of arms and armour. With paste-boards and silver paper pasted on them, the crowns of sola hats, coloured cotton wool for the crest and helmet and Latin mottos on the shields, we managed the show somehow. But the play was a great success......... It was during the staging of *Chandragupta* by the Institute members that Sisir Kumar made a hit in the role of Chanakya. For this play also the costumes were evolved by the members.'

Dr Chatterjee also rendered invaluable assistance in the designing of costumes for the play *Sita* which caused such a stir in the Bengali stage. For this mythological play he made sketches of costumes and adornments that would vividly suggest to the audience the great days of the ancient Hindu period in India. On the basis of these sketches and from ideas derived from drawings by the artist Charu Roy, the costumes for Sita were made out of costly material secured at great expense from places in the far South, Surat, Ajmere, etc. When the play was staged these costumes served so effectively to conjure up the atmosphere of ancient India that one critic remarked –

> 'Sisir Kumar by his careful preparation and selection of costumes authentic to the ancient Hindu era and so pleasing to the eye has rounded off the play most admirably.'

This performance so delighted Rabindranath Tagore that he enthusiastically declared: 'I have the very greatest respect for Sisir Kumar Bhaduri's exceptional talent as a producer' (Letter to Monilal Ganguli, 2nd Bhadra 1331).

When arranging to stage *Alamgir*, the producer conducted the most vigorous research and carefully studied all the most reliable literatures relating to the period so as to give a faithful presentation of that inimitable and awe-inspiring Mughal Emperor and to ensure that the costumes both of the leading characters as also of the Mughal and Rajput women who appeared should be correct in every detail. As a further measure in this regard he visited the premises of his distinguished friend Bahadur Singh Singhee, whose celebrated collections of Indian works of art was widely known and carefully studied numerous Mughal and Rajput paintings. Another great friend of Sisir Kumar Bhaduri, Rakhaldas Banerjee, so well known in the scholarly circle, also lent his assistance for Emperor Alamgir and other Muslim characters, and also gave clear directions as to the costumes worn in those days by Rajput rulers of Jodhpur, Jaipur etc. even going into such details as the subtle distinctions in regard to the way that they bound their turbans. As a result of all this, the final costumes prepared for the performance of *Alamgir* were correct down to the last detail. Embroidered Nagra slippers to be worn by Alamgir were secured from distant Peshawar, the cost of three pairs running to the astounding figure of about one hundred and fifty rupees. Rakhaldas also gave invaluable advice in other matters beside that of costumes. For example, when attending a rehearsal on one occasion, he gave precise directions as to how courtiers saluted the Emperor in those days. The left hand would be raised to the turban, and the courtier would bow down and bring his right hand near the ground. He also explained the origin of this type of salute. He said that, in the days when Akbar was Emperor, Prince Selim once came up to make his obeisance. Bowing low before the throne he suddenly felt his turban slipping and so he hurriedly brought up his left hand to keep it steady and supported himself by bringing his right hand down to the ground. The whole effect was so pleasing to the Emperor that he decreed that this should be the form of salutation in future at all Mughal durbars. Such was the care that producer Bhaduri would take in regard to small details so as to ensure the success of any play he produced.

Again while staging a performance of that excellent play of Tagore—*Tapati*, he was keenly attentive to the details of the costumes to be worn by the characters in this play, and took infinite pains in this regard. His friend Rakhaldas Banerjee collected a number of useful items for him. When Sisir Kumar Bhaduri heard that a friend was proceeding to Kashmir – quite inaccessible in those days – he requested him to secure from there authentic Kashmiri costumes and other articles of various kinds, for which he made over a substantial sum of money. The friend availed himself of the assistance of the then superintendent of the Raja Amar Sing Technical School and returned with an imposing array of Kashmiri costumes, thrones with Kashmiri decorations, gabba, etc. It is clear that Sisir Kumar Bhaduri would spare no expense to ensure that the plays he staged should not lack appropriate costumes, jewellery, etc. On the occasion described above, the cost of the costumes and fittings far exceeded the entire box office receipts, but this did not worry Sisir Kumar Bhaduri. For he had been determined to put on a play worthy in every respect, and Rabindranath himself was delighted at the performance.

Bisarjan is another celebrated play by Tagore. This was staged more than once by the poet himself and he played the roles of Joy Sinha and Raghupati. No one in those days could even imagine, however, that anyone would venture to put on the professional stage such difficult plays as *Tapati* or *Bisarjan*. Nevertheless, that outstanding artiste Sisir Kumar Bhaduri, on whom Rabindranath himself once bestowed the glorious title of *Nataraj*, did take on the ambitious task of staging *Bisarjan* and the performance was a great success. This play is concerned with Tripura state. Before staging it Sisir Kumar Bhaduri went along with his friend Monilal Ganguli to see the Bara Thakur of Tripura state, from whom he gathered exhaustive information regarding the costumes and customs of that state, even to the extent of full particulars regarding the attires of the ladies of the royal palace. On the basis of this and other information the exquisite costumes of Raja Gobindo Manikya, Rani Gunabati, Joy Sinha, Raghupati etc. were prepared. On the night of the performance the actors and actresses came on the stage attired in the carefully selected and attractive costumes that impressed the audiences with their authenticity almost as much as did the excellent quality of the acting.

Sisir Kumar Bhaduri's production of Jogesh Chandra Chowdhuri's *Digbijoyi* furnishes another example of his unrivalled skill as a producer. The acting, the scenery and the costumes all combined to fascinate and amaze the audience. The impression created upon them that night was one they could never forget. In this instance, too, Sisir Kumar Bhaduri was required to take infinite pains in the selection of suitable costumes. He earnestly studied all the most authoritative historical works relating to the hero of the play, Nadir Shah, Emperor of Persia, and other characters. In search of suitable books and pictures he would pay a daily visit to the Asiatic Society Library and the Imperial Library (now the National Library). He discussed matters with those friends of his who were distinguished historians, and sought their advice. Those who attended the performance could hardly have imagined what indefatigable efforts and what vast sums of money had been involved in presenting to them on the stage a faithful representation of the great Persian monarch. Quite apart from the excellent quality of the acting, no pains had been spared to ensure that there should not be a single jarring note in the costumes, scenery or any other stage detail. Brocades from Banaras costing many thousands of rupees and expensive furs from Kashmir had been procured for the preparation of appropriate costumes for Nadir Shah, Saler Beg, Sitara etc. Clad in these costumes admirably set off by the exquisite backdrops painted by the skilled artists Johur and Ramendranath, the impression created on the audiences by the stage cast must have been that of historical characters coming truly alive.

A great deal more could be said that would clearly demonstrate how unfailingly scrupulous producer Bhaduri was in the selection of stage costumes. Space will not permit further dissertations in this regard. But there can be no doubt that what Dr P. Guha Thakurta said of him is absolutely true. He remarked –

> 'He is a thorough student of modern European stag-craft, and judging from his very recent productions, notably those of "*Alamgir*", "*Sita*", "*Sorosi*" and "*Roma*", the last two being social plays dramatised from the original novels of Mr. Sarat Chandra

> Chatterjee, Mr. Bhaduri has shown distinct originality in the art of production. He attends to accuracy of detail and perfection of technique. He keeps his eye on the setting against which his men and women are to stand and he knows how to handle his material so as to produce a harmony between the play and its atmosphere. He does not employ the stock-in-trade of the older stage -practitioners, and he is developing a new style of the new age.' (*The Bengali Drama*, by Dr P. Guha Thakurta).

Another very just tribute was also paid to producer Sisir Kumar Bhaduri. It ran thus –

> 'There is no room for contradiction today that Mr. Bhaduri's position as a producer is unapproachable.' (*Sisir Kumar Bhaduri as a producer* by Ranganath).

It is for this reason that not merely our own supreme poet and dramatic critic, Rabindranath, but the most distinguished artists and art critics from abroad such as Sir L. Casson, Dame Sybil Thorndyke, Pudovkin, Dr Rosamond Gilder, etc. were invariably most favourably impressed by the performances at Sisir Kumar Bhaduri's theatre, and could hardly praise him enough.

First published in *Puja Annual, Hindustan Standard*, 1959

STAGE DÉCOR OF SISIR KUMAR BHADURI

STAGE DÉCOR OF SISIR KUMAR BHADURI

It is only on the stage that literature and the fine arts come into intimate association. A successful stage performance depends upon the expert prowess of the dramatist, the actors and actresses, the scene painters, the musicians and the dancers. It is for this reason that, when putting on a play, India's first and foremost producer Sisir Kumar Bhaduri would not concentrate merely on the acting but would keep a careful eye on all these other components of a successful performance. This article will deal with some of the distinguished artists, who under the inspired direction of Sisir Kumar Bhaduri, brought about drastic and unimaginable changes to the realm of stage furnishing and scenery on the professional stage, thus ushering in a new era.

It is hardly necessary to mention that the Bengali stage was built up in imitation of the English theatres in Calcutta. As a result, the stage settings and scenery followed for a long period the pattern of the western stage. Consequently, natural scenery, palaces, gardens etc were all drawn on flat scenes let down from above. These unnatural and unsightly scenes were described by Antoine as 'ridiculous backdrops which have no atmosphere or depth.'

Both in Europe and America a number of changes have taken place in the technique of stage furnishing and scenery alongside the stage developments generally, and considerable improvement has been effected. These improvements have been brought about by the earnest efforts of numerous gifted people connected with the stage and this activity has maintained uninterrupted progress. Discussing this progress on the English stage Allardyee Nicoll remarks.

> '..... from Kemble, through Macready and Charles Kean, on to Irving and Tree is one steady line of progression', (*The English Stage*.)

There were many who did not hesitate to spend vast sums in the promotion of this effort. It may be noted that towards the end of the 19th century, at a performance of *Henry VIII 'the settings alone cost over £10,000.'* Later, the highly gifted Edward Gordon Craig and Adolph Appia contributed substantially to improvements in this field and have earned a place of honour in the annals of the European stage.

In spite of many sporadic attempts at improving the stage performances in Bengal, the technique of stage furnishing and scenery was still in its infancy right up to the second decade of the present century. It was that superb producer Sisir Kumar Bhaduri who brought about drastic changes in this sphere when putting on a performance of *Sita*. These radical changes amazed the stage lovers of the time and will always be remembered by historians of the stage. Regarding the exceptional care that Sisir Kumar Bhaduri took to ensure that the furnishings and scenery were in all respects appropriate to the action of the play Dr P. Guha Thakurta remarked–

> 'He keeps his eye on the setting against which his men and women are to stand and he knows how to handle his material so as to produce a harmony between the play and its atmosphere.' (*The Bengali Drama*).

A genius himself, he collected a number of distinguished artists around him who were not associated with theatres in general and therefore unaffected by the traditional techniques. The distinguished dramatic critic Hemendra Kumar Roy in his *Bangla Rangalaya O Sisir Kumar*, said about them that they were all quite familiar with Sisir Kumar Bhaduri's plans and ideas. Therefore, each working independently in his own sphere. They yet succeeded in producing the most harmonious results.

Pre-eminent among these was the renowned artist Charu Roy whose unrivalled skill with the brush brought about a revolutionary change in Bengali stage décor. A devotee of Indian art, Charu Roy was a pupil of Silpacharya Abanindranath Tagore. His hauntingly beautiful paintings have been widely praised in India and abroad. This is only natural as beside his skill as a painter, his inborn, poetic qualities and exquisite taste lend distinction to his work. It was to this distinguished artist that Sisir Kumar Bhaduri entrusted the design of the scenery and stage furnishings for the performance of *Sita*.

How apt was the producer's choice was amply demonstrated when the play was put on. The distinguished dramatic critic Dr P. Guha Thakurta remarked –

> 'So far the best and most convincingly realistic painting and designing for the stage have been done by Mr. Charu Roy in the productions at Mr. Sisir Kumar Bhaduri's Natya-Mandir.' (*The Bengali Drama*).

Before taking up his task Charu Roy held long consultation with the celebrated archaeologist Rakhaldas Banerjee, Dr Suniti Kumar Chatterjee and other authorities in regard to the architecture of ancient India and the modes thereof. He also consulted the appropriate books on the subject and made an earnest study of the architectural designs of ancient India from available illustrations. Prior to this he had visited in numerous places the sites where specimens of ancient architectures had been discovered and had made careful drawings of these. Before finalising his plans he also read the *Ramayana* repeatedly. It might be remarked that Charu Roy, under the direction of Sisir Kumar Bhaduri, started planning the stage sets and scenery for the performance of *Sita* before the play itself was complete.

In a review published in a paper at that time (*Nautchghar*, 3rd Aswin 1331 BS) the above-mentioned dramatic critic Hemendra Kumar Roy said of Charu Roy's stage settings and scenery that their originality was really outstanding. He went on to express his firm belief that the radical departure from tradition in the designing of the scenery had ushered in a new age for the Bengali theatre and that Charu Roy's place was assured in the annals of the Bengali stage. This is a very correct judgment. The gifted artist did indeed initiate a new era with his stage scenery and settings. The unnatural flat scenes with false perspectives found no place in Charu Roy's designs but were replaced by what are known in stage circles as 'set scenes.' This is the first time that three-dimension representation appeared on the Bengali stage, and the houses, palaces and gardens presented a most natural appearance. There was not a single path or door depicted on the scenery which could not be used by members of the cast, truly a combination of the beautiful and the realistic in stage sets.

Stage lighting is very important to the natural appearance of stage scenery and Charu Roy accordingly paid due attention to this sphere also. Switching off the unglamorous, artificial and unpleasant illumination of the footlights he arranged for stage lighting from the top and the sides. This had been practiced for many years in Europe and America, but it was the first time it had been tried here.

It would perhaps be appropriate to say a few words about his remarkable skill as a painter. So apt were the scenes his brush created that the atmosphere of that remote age described in the *Ramayana* was vividly evoked. His stage sets and scenery were as fascinating as the superb performance of the actors and actresses taking part in this performance of *Sita*, and the appreciative audience was spellbound. The critic remarked that never before in the history of the Bengali stage had such exquisite skill been devoted to the painting of the scenery. Nowhere in the scenes was any sign of carelessness or excess observed. Abanindranath Tagore expressed the opinion that—'Charu Roy is a most skilful artist, he has devoted great care to the design of the stage furnishings and the scenery.'

An interesting fact might here be recorded which only a few of Sisir Kumar Bhaduri's intimate associates know about. Some people expressed doubts as to whether the stage scenery painted by Charu Roy really depicted the authentic architectural features of the period of the *Ramayana*. Attentive to the minutest detail of all aspects of a stage performance Sisir Kumar Bhaduri decided to call in Abanindranath Tagore to point out any defects he might observe in these stage scenes. It is hardly necessary to mention that in spite of all the money and care that had been devoted to the preparation of these stage scenes, Sisir Kumar Bhaduri would not have hesitated an instant to reject them had any error been discovered. Charu Roy too would have gladly scrapped these stage scenes on which he had labored so assiduously had they proved faulty, and started his work afresh. But this was not necessary. Abanindranath was delighted with the design and skillful drawings of the scenes. In answer to the adverse critics he remarked that the actual period of the *Ramayana* had not yet been determined and that no specimens of the architecture of the time had been discovered. He said he considered that the stage décor undoubtedly brought to mind the ancient historical period of the Hindu era, and that, in his opinion, was adequate. Bhaduri also expressed the view that the settings were suggestive only. The adverse critics were silenced by these irrefutable arguments of Abanindranath and Sisir Kumar Bhaduri. Rakhaldas Banerjee and others expressed themselves as entirely in agreement with Abanindranath.

There is another matter worth mentioning in this connection. Although Charu Roy's stage scenery could not serve the purpose of having such an enormous stage at New York, they were greatly admired by observers who were much impressed by the *Hindu artist*'s exceptional skill.

And now a few words about another of Sisir Kumar Bhaduri's most able and famous artists Ramendranath Chatterjee. He too had had the good fortune of being trained by Abanindranath Tagore. His paintings so attractively executed, earned the praise and admiration of well-known connoisseurs of art both here and abroad. His picture of unblemished beauty *Upashika* executed with all the tender grace of his peculiar style was greatly admired in Germany.

Ramendranath was attracted to the professional stage by the glittering talents of Sisir Kumar Bhaduri and soon earned a reputation as a stage decorator of outstanding ability. Both his designs and his brushwork were of a very high order. His stage scenery and settings for the popular play *Digbijoyee* were highly praised by the editor of *Nautchghar* who remarked in this connection –

> 'The scenery and settings of *Digbijoyee* are outstanding in a unique fashion. The impression gained is that they are

> of a type never before seen elsewhere. Not merely are they of exceptional artistic merit displaying exquisite taste, but are a new creation altogether.' (*Nautchghar*, 20th Pous 1335 BS).

The great artist unquestionably displayed in his work both intimate knowledge of his *métier* and highly developed taste. Whilst presenting a most realistic appearance his scenes were nowhere lacking in beauty. In the camp scene of *Nadir Shah* the artist displayed on the stage an enormous tent from which the exit path was depicted emerging and dissolving in the distance. Some smaller tents were shown on both sides. It was a most attractive scene that members of the audience must vividly remember right up to the present day, and that most skillfully designed and executed path shown, vanishing in the distance was particularly impressive.

Another outstanding scene is worth of mention. This depicted the courtyard of the Ruknadaulla mosque situated in Chandney Chowk in Delhi. At first sight it seemed unimpressive. When however, Nadir Shah issues his cruel edict for the slaying of the citizens of Delhi, the superb artistry woven into this apparently commonplace scene becomes apparent. As the triumphant shouts of the victors and wailing of the vanquished mingled with the sounds of the drums and bugles are heard, the scene is suddenly lit up with a dazzling spark of flame, vividly suggesting the horrible scenes of butchery taking place in the city. The dazzling sparks rising to the skies and lighting up the scenery were a most adroit device of the artist to stir the emotion of the audience, causing them to feel both fear and pity.

Ramendranath was entrusted with the designing of the scenery and stage sets for the performance of that popular tropical play *Shahjahan*. No better choice could have been made.

So appropriate were the scenes and settings that the splendor and magnificence of that vanished age were vividly evoked in the minds of the audience. No detailed description is possible in the brief space of this article but one particular scene simply must be touched upon. That is the scene of the Taj Mahal, that expression of a dream in white marble on the opposite bank of the Jumna, which serves as a superb symbol of Shahjahan's great love for his wife. Only a truly talented artist could adequately depict on a stage scene this world-renowned edifice. Both the design and execution were flawless, and the scene would amaze the audience. Rakhaldas Banerjee was particularly impressed by this scene, so much so that when congratulating the artist he said that he had only known of one Taj Mahal before he saw this scene, and now knew of two. What greater praise could any artist receive from so distinguished an archaeologist?

Stage historians will constantly refer to the outstanding contributions, in the form of scenery, that Rabindranath had gifted to stage performances of plays such as *Sorosi*, *Bisarjan*, *Shyama*, *Tapati* and many more.

That celebrated Indian artist Jamini Roy, equally famous both here and abroad, also designed some stage scenes under Sisir Kumar Bhaduri's direction. His distinctive blending of line and colour is familiar to every art lover. It is, therefore, hardly necessary to say more than that some of the scenes he designed and executed for a stage performance of *Sarama* will live forever in the minds of those who were privileged to see them.

A few words should be said about Johur, who has already been mentioned above in connection with Ramendranath. Sisir Kumar Bhaduri would often speak of this talented artist, and said of him that though he was undistinguished as a designer, his skill as a painter was hard to match. Such was the magic of Johur's brush work that audiences would frequently take his painted scenes to be real. He excelled above all at landscape painting. Wholly dedicated to art and a tireless worker, Johur could paint a beautiful and faultless scene in a few hours, so great was his skill. His scenes lent authenticity and beauty to a great many plays staged in those days at the Natyamandir. The temple of Martyanda in *Tapati* and the temple of *Bhubaneswari* in *Bisarjan* are specimens of his work which stand unrivalled in their beauty of execution and singularly appropriate line, and colour. The scene he painted of the old house in Bagbazar described in *Shes-raksa* truly amazed the audience. They could hardly believe that the cracked walls and white-ant infested doors and windows depicted on the scene could have been painted. The scenery he painted for a performance of *Hasu-no-hana* was another outstanding example of his skill as a painter. The streets, gardens and pagoda-shaped houses of Japan were most fascinating. Many other examples could be cited but space does not permit.

Mention should be made of *Potua*s such as Binode, Rajen and Nilmony etc. who assisted the above-mentioned artists in their work.

In conclusion I shall like to add that it was Sisir Kumar Bhaduri's practice when putting on a new play to have its symbol painted on the two front wings of the stage. In the case of *Sita* the symbol was two white lotuses, in the case of *Digbijoyee* two Persian minars and so forth. When the *Srirangam Theatre* was opened with a performance of *Jivanranga* symbols representing life and death were painted in cubistic style on the two front wings. It was the well-known artist Promode Kumar Chatterjee who drew these.

First published in *Puja Annual, Hindustan Standard*, 1961

SISIR KUMAR BHADURI IN THE EYES OF FOREIGNERS

SISIR KUMAR BHADURI IN THE EYES OF FOREIGNERS

It was in the year 1795 that the very first Bengali theatre was established in Calcutta. The founder of this theatre Heresim Lebedeff, a Russian, has himself placed on record that his main object in setting up this theatre was to provide entertainment for the Europeans in the city. It is fairly safe to assume, therefore, that among the audiences at the performances at this theatre were quite a number of English people resident in Calcutta at that time. It would also be logical to deduce that what induced most of these English people to attend the performances at this theatre was the desire to lend a little novelty to their daily life in a country far removed from home, as few of them could have hoped to gain genuine aesthetic enjoyment from stage performances in a language completely strange to them. Unfortunately, however, for some reason or other, the theatre closed down for good after performances had been staged for two nights only. A long period was to elapse after that before anyone gave any serious attention to the question of setting up another Bengali theatre in Calcutta.

The 18th century had given way to the 19th before highly educated Bengalis of the upper classes, such as Prasanna Kumar Tagore, Nabin Chandra Bose, Sarat Chandra Ghose, Kaliprasanna Sinha,

Raja Pratap Chandra Sinha, Raja Iswar Chandra Sinha, Maharaja Jyotindra Mohon Tagore, Jyotirindranath Tagore, Gunendranath Tagore and others, following the example of the English in Calcutta, began to set up theatres in the city. Small theatres were also built at the various Bengali educational institutions. Newspaper reports of the period testify to the fact that distinguished English citizens of Calcutta including high-ranking officials such as Sir Edward Ryan, Horace Hayman Wilson, J. P. Grant, Lord Northbrook and others would often attend performances at these various Bengali theatres established at different times. All of them, however, would come as guests of the wealthy and highly-placed Bengali families who arranged amateur stage performances purely for their own diversion.

It was after the opening of the first professional Bengali theatre in the year 1872 that a number of other public theatres came into being. Only once in a while would a few English people be found among the audiences at these theatres. It was not until the 20th century that English people started regularly attending performances at Bengali theatres and were genuinely anxious to savour to the full the qualities of the plays put on. It would certainly be no exaggeration to assert that the vast majority of these were in the habit of attending performances at Sisir Kumar Bhaduri's theatre. Soon after he entered on his professional stage career, reports of the outstanding genius of this born artiste began to spread far and wide. He could well have said in Caesar's words, '*Vini, Vidi, Vici*'. He soon attracted the favourable attention of such outstanding figures of the time as Rabindranath, Harapasad Sastri, Desbhandu Chittaranjan Das, Abanindranath Tagore etc., and he was fortunate enough to earn their unstinted praise. It was not long before reports of his exceptional qualities as an actor were carried to scholars and lovers of the stage abroad. Many were the celebrated artistes, authors and dramatic critics of numerous Western nations who found their way to the auditorium of his theatre. Among these were Russians, Americans, English, German, French, etc. All were entranced by the superb quality of his acting and were most lavish in their spontaneous praise of the greatest stage star this country has ever produced.

What is more, a performance of *Sita* by Sisir Kumar Bhaduri in 1928 was instrumental in bringing about his subsequent appearance on the New York stage. Flight Lieutenant E.B. Elliot of the Royal Air Force happened to be at the theatre and was so favourably impressed by the play, every single aspect as detail of which had been so carefully planned and fitted together as to ensure an outstandingly successful performance, that to quote the newspaper report – 'After the second act Elliott asked to be taken to the actor-manager's dressing room where he said simply; "*I realize I am in the presence of a very great artist*". Thereafter he never missed a play at Sisir Bhaduri's theatre right up to the time when he had to return to his own country. He came back to Calcutta a year later and was constantly to be seen at performances at Sisir Kumar Bhaduri's theatre, Natyamandir, which he would follow with rapt attention. He left again for home and nothing was heard of him for a long time. Later Sisir Kumar Bhaduri received a letter from New York offering *India's Greatest Actor* a New York engagement. Elliot arrived in Calcutta at about the same time and soon all the formalities relating to the contract were completed. Sisir Kumar Bhaduri sailed for New York with his troupe in 1930.'

The following newspaper report will serve to illustrate the warmth of the welcome accorded to our great actor in the United States.

> 'As they lay outside the harbor at night, watching the myriad lights of the twinkling sky scraper skyline, a page boy came

> down the deck with a message to say that S. K. Bhaduri had been granted a *Mayor's reception* on his arrival at the point of landing. With the coming of the day-break, any doubts the party had as to the meaning of this were soon dispelled. The *Mayor's reception committee*, headed by the Grand Duchess Marie of Russia and Princess Rospigliosi came aboard and shortly afterwards the whole company, in *dhoti*s and *sari*s just as they had left Calcutta, were being driven down Broadway at breakneck speed in six Rolls Royce motor cars preceded by motor cycle police with screaming sirens.
>
> During the whirlwind weeks that followed, rehearsals were interposed by visits to the Broadway theatres. Wherever the company went special police were on duty to hold back the crowds of excited people, anxious to catch a glimpse of the celebrated Bengalis'.

As a result of various, unexpected developments, the tour did not prove a great success financially. A study of the newspaper reports, however, make it abundantly clear his actual stage performances were very well received and, from that point of view, his visit to New York must be regarded as being well worthwhile. For example *The New York Sun* reported as follows:

> 'The Hindu players made a very good impression. Their acting compares favourably with the acting of any foreign troupe I can think of, excepting, of course, the Moscow Art Theatres players, who, to me at least, are the best actors in the world. The Hindu players are so graceful in their movements that their many gestures are never awkward. They speak their lines clearly and distinctly, even if one does not know what they are saying. And the star, Mr. Bhaduri, who plays *Rama*, is an emotional actor of considerable power….. There is a certain nobility inherent in this play, and this nobility even pervaded the acting. Doubtless this was because the love theme is on such a high plane. One

> had the feeling that the love of *Rama* and *Sita* would persist through all eternity'.

Then again *The New York American* said:

> 'Novelty came to the current theatrical season at the *Vanderbilt Theatre* last night in perhaps the most ancient play that has been shown on Broadway... This company of Hindu actors, speaking in language so distinctly foreign to American ears, succeeded in vitalizing this story to such an extent that scarily a person left before the final curtain. After all, beauty and anguish know no tongue. There is a universal language, and art their sole medium of expression. The beauty of the poetry, the anguish of the King *Rama* and his Queen were too real to escape transmission over the footlights on the wings of an artistry rare to this country.....
>
> Sisir Kumar Bhaduri is an actor of the finest rank. Last night play kept him in two contrasting moods – lyric and emotion. He seemed to excel in the latter, investing some of his scenes with a poignancy that strongly moved his audience. The supporting cast was almost equally strong, the women particularly'.

The year previous to Bhaduri's visit to New York had seen the appearance on that city's stage of dramatic troupes from China and Japan. In the opinion of the dramatic critic of *The Daily News New York*, however, Sisir Kumar Bhaduri's performances had proved far more comprehensible to the New York audiences and struck them as being of a higher order altogether than the plays staged by the Chinese and Japanese companies. He writes as follows:

> 'The players reveal themselves as handsome and graceful in their bright robes and spangles, and their language as a mellifluous one. Spoken as it was last night, it often has the quality of a song – a melody of more variety and depth than, for instance, the sing song of China's Me-Lan-Fang.

> As actors Bhaduri and his company are more easily understood than were the Chinese and Japanese last season. Their gestures and vocal inflections are readily divined and the performances are generally emotional.'

It is also made abundantly clear in the review that appeared in *The Evening World* that the fact that the plays were presented in a language strange to the audience did not prove by any means an insuperable bar to their understanding and appreciation on the part of New York audiences. The dramatic critic of the paper remarks as follows:

> 'Of course there were few in the audience who understood the language of the visitors. But that mattered little. So superb was their pantomime, so illustrative was a shrug of the shoulders, a flash of the eye, and a lifting of the hands or arms, that one could follow the story with little trouble....
>
> It was a treat to watch Sisir Kumar Bhaduri as *Rama*. His voice was bell-like; his pantomime, which told the story as clearly to the audience which understood not a single word, was so perfect that the words anyway, would have been unnecessary. Excellent too, was Sreemati Prova as *Sita*, the Queen. All the others in the cast were interesting...
>
> It might not harm many who take the stage as their profession to drop into the Vanderbilt to see how strangers in a strange land, speaking a strange language to their patrons, can through their pantomime, interpret a story so that, as pointed out, the verbal picture is unnecessary.
>
> You'll enjoy *Sita* as something unique.'

Another paper, besides bestowing lavish praise on the outstanding histrionic abilities of Sisir Kumar Bhaduri and the other members of his company, went on to say such complimentary things about the language, songs, dances etc., of Bengal that it is impossible to resist the temptation to set it all down here. The review went on to say that the performance of *Sita* had made the audience enthusiastic about all things Indian. To quote from the beautifully phrased review:

> 'The star of this company is undoubtedly an actor of great ability and his supporting company seem to take their work very seriously, portraying each role, large or small, with great emphasis, conviction and many gestures. Then too, there is something quite musical and pleasant about the sound of the language. The native songs and dances were particularly interesting.
>
> Sita further arouses one's curiosity about India and at least presents a picture of what goes on in Sisir Bhaduri's Theatre in Calcutta.' (*The Evening Graphic New York*).

Due to the currency to this day of vague reports, partly accurate and partly fictitious, regarding Bhaduri's professional tour of the States the whole affair is still shrouded in mystery for a good many people. It is for this reason that I considered it appropriate to quote extensively from the New York papers.

Soon after his return to India Sisir Kumar Bhaduri had the unique privilege of being required by the Viceroy of India, Lord Irwin, to give a command performance in Delhi. The play Sita was staged in the presence of the Viceroy, a large number of princes, high-ranking Government officials and other distinguished people. The audience followed the play with rapt attention right up to the time when the curtain descended at the close of the last scene. Summoning the great stage artists and director Sisir Kumar Bhaduri the Viceroy shook him warmly by the hand and expressed his keen appreciation of the play and his gratitude for the pains he had taken. He also shook hands with and congratulated the other members of the company. Moreover, the Military Secretary to the Viceroy addressed Sisir

Kumar Bhaduri the letter quoted below on 21st March 1931 expressing formal thanks on behalf of the Viceroy. He wrote:

D. O. No. 1882
The Viceroy's House, New Delhi
The 21st March, 1931
Military Secretary, To The Viceroy.

Dear Mr Bhaduri,
I am desired by their Excellencies to tell you how much they enjoyed your performance last night. It was a consummate piece of acting and the greatest praise is due not only to you yourself who took the principal part, but also to all the rest of your cast.

The fact that we were able to follow the play although we could not understand a word of the language, in itself says much for the acting. Their Excellencies were quite thrilled with it and desire me to offer you their warm congratulations.

Yours faithfully,
Sd. Lt. Col. C. O. Hurvey
M.S.V.

At one time there was a very long run of the play *Sita* but audiences did not tire of it. Every single performance was played to a packed house and many who could not secure tickets were turned away disappointed. At that period a number of English people were to be found among the audiences at Sisir Kumar Bhaduri's theatre and not merely for the performance of *Sita* but for numerous other plays staged by him as well. Among English members of the audience were High Court Judges, eminent barristers and high-ranking members of the Civil Service. Mr Justice Lord Williams was most favourably impressed by *Sita* and wrote a letter expressing his appreciation to a common friend of his and Sisir Kumar Bhaduri's, a well-known solicitor of the High Court.

As has been mentioned earlier in the article, it was not merely the English residents of Calcutta who would visit Sisir Kumar Bhaduri's theatre but also great many distinguished people from the U.S.A. and numerous European countries. In the fifties of this century, the Russian Cultural Mission consisting of such distinguished people as Pudovkin, Cherkasov etc., toured India and, in the course of their tour, visited Calcutta. They were in the city for only a very short period, but in spite of a packed schedule they did not omit to pay a visit to Sisir Kumar Bhaduri's theatre to see our great artiste in one of his performances. Sudhi Pradhan of the Indo-Soviet Cultural Society contacted Sisir Kumar Bhaduri and made all arrangements for the reception of these distinguished visitors. On the appointed evening Pudovkin, Cherkasov and others came along with Sudhi Pradhan, Hiren Mukherjee and an interpreter, a Russian lady. The ever-popular play *Sorosi* by that great writer Sarat Chandra Chatterjee was presented.

In spite of the fact that the play was performed in a language they could not understand these distinguished foreign visitors waxed enthusiastic after only a few scenes. Once more that gifted artiste and director Sisir Kumar Bhaduri, the adornment and pride of the Bengali stage, demonstrated that in spite of the language difficulty he was able to get across to foreigners in the audience the full qualities and all the beauties of the Bengali plays he presented and captured their enthusiasm. Pudovkin whispered to Sudhi Pradhan that it would be impossible for them to leave the theatre until they had followed the play right up to the end. He also requested him to convey a message to the appropriate quarters that they would not be able to attend the dinner at which they were expected. They sat still as marble, their eyes intent on each succeeding scene and the brilliant stage performance, completely entranced by the entertainment. The pathetic last scene of the tragedy was played and then the curtain descended.

Pudovkin, Cherkasov and others were most anxious to meet Sisir Kumar Bhaduri. They were taken to his dressing room. Each one of the visitors shook hands warmly with Sisir Kumar Bhaduri. Pudovkin could speak English and he said 'You are a great artiste.' Weary after his long hours on the stage Sisir Kumar Bhaduri just smiled slightly. Silence followed which was broken by Pudovkin who asked – 'Do you know why you are great?' Sisir Kumar Bhaduri was completely taken aback by this unexpected and delicate question and modestly made no response. Pudovkin then answered his own question. He said –

> 'The moment you come on to the stage you capture the attention of the audience. Then while you are establishing the character you portray they relax somewhat after the first attraction. As the play proceeds, however, your every gesture and intonation strike at them. After a while they lose all sense of individuality and personal preference. They become completely fascinated as it were and then, like some master magician, you can present them with any character you choose to depict and they will accept it as completely authentic.'

This is a beautiful and most accurate description of the dramatic genius of that born artist Sisir Kumar Bhaduri. Only a dramatic critic of so high an order as Pudovkin could possibly phrase so accurate an appraisal in a few words after seeing but one performance. He finally remarked that Sisir Kumar Bhaduri's acting was based upon a firm, realistic principle.

Cherkasov had only one remark to make. He referred to the one thing that amazed and pained him, namely that an actor of Sisir Kumar Bhaduri's calibre should have to act in the type of theatre and in the sordid atmosphere to which he was confined. Sisir Kumar Bhaduri then thanked his guests profusely for their congratulations and for the kind things they had said. In regard to Pudovkin's last pronouncement he stated that the dramatic art of India had all along been based on a firm, realistic principle. He went on to say that it would be wrong for them to assume that this was his individual contribution to the Bengali stage. This was fresh proof to his intimate circle of friends, who were present there, of his intense patriotism, of which of course they were well aware. He would never dream of trying to add to his own reputation by belittling any institution or tradition connected with the Indian stage. In answer to Cherkasov's remark he made a characteristic statement which his fellow-countrymen, particularly his devoted audiences will never forget. He said—'The people of my country are fond of me, and it is their affection and sympathy that have kept me and my theatre going. You are probably aware of the great poverty that prevails in our country. This poverty is reflected in the poverty of my own theatre'. He went on to say—'In your country the State will lend support to the stage whenever necessary. That is not the case here. A theatre in this country must stand on its own feet.'

Sisir Kumar Bhaduri has been in the front line in maintaining the theatrical performances of high standards in universities and colleges of the then contemporary period.

When shaking hands before leaving, Pudovkin said, 'We hope to meet you again.' To this Cherkasov added, 'At Moscow or Leningad.' These were no mere figures of speech. The Russians truly and sincerely hoped and believed that they would soon see Sisir Kumar Bhaduri in Russia. Shortly after their return to Russia Sisir Kumar Bhaduri received an invitation through the Russian Embassy to visit the U.S.S.R. For various reasons he was not able to avail himself of the opportunity of visiting Russia. Moreover, the Russian artistes, on their return to their motherland, wrote about their experiences of their Indian tour in the renowned paper *Pravda*, and made extensive references to Sisir Kumar Bhaduri and his theatre, as also did Cherkasov in his book on the Indian tour.

It might here be appropriate to refer to the incident of another evening when another foreigner came to see a performance of *Sorosi*. A German visitor came suddenly one day to see the play. He followed it with careful attention from start to finish. He knew not a syllable of Bengali, but that made no difference. The highly skilled acting of Sisir Kumar Bhaduri and his company enabled him to follow the action with ease. At the end of the performance the newly arrived foreign visitor to the theatre praised Sisir Kumar Bhaduri effusively. With a lurking smile he then went on to tell the great actor the impressions he had received as to the play's message. He said that to him it seemed tinged with communistic ideas and advocated that the land should belong to the cultivators. The superb quality of the acting conveyed clearly to a member of the audience the full purport of the play despite the fact that it was performed in a language totally strange to him. It might be appropriate to remark in this connection that it was precisely because the play does put forward these ideas that Sisir Kumar Bhaduri selected *Sorosi* for his performance the night the members of the Russian Cultural Mission were present at his theatre.

The members of *Chinese Goodwill Mission*, as guests of the West Bengal Government, also came to see one of his stage performances. The play performed that night was *Takht-e-Taus* which is about Jahandar Shah, a grandson of Alamgir, who occupied the Peacock Throne of the Mughal Empire, which was shortly to collapse, for just a few months. Jahandar Shah's character was of a startlingly contradictory nature; while whimsical, pleasure-loving, uncultured and even wicked in some ways he yet had a deep religious faith and was most respectful towards virtuous and saintly people. So convincing was Sisir Kumar Bhaduri's portrayal of this complex character that the distinguished Chinese guests were amazed and deeply impressed. The performance gave them the utmost satisfaction.

Another distinguished foreigner, who greatly enjoyed an performance of Sisir Kumar Bhaduri, which he happened to attend, was the Art Director of Paris Opera House—the famous French institution, so well known throughout Europe. Before leaving the theatre he assured Bhaduri that he would carry home with him the happiest memories of that evening's performance.

A few words would now be appropriate concerning the meeting between that world-renowned couple of the English stage Sir Lewis Casson and Dame Sybil Thorndike and their subsequent visit to his theatre to see him on the stage. Sir Lewis and his highly distinguished wife are so well known that no account is here necessary of their outstanding achievements on the stage. In the year 1954 they passed through Calcutta on their way to Australia. The British Council arranged a small tea-party at which they were introduced to our great actor Sisir Kumar Bhaduri. The writer was also present at this function and therefore had the privilege of listening to the conversation between the stage celebrities of the West and the East, some of which is now related. They were delighted to meet each other and over tea discussed a wide variety of subjects ranging from the *Jatra*s of ancient days right up to present-day theatre, the problems the latter are facing and possible means of overcoming them. Other topics discussed related to the cinema, open air theatre, and a great many other subjects besides. It became abundantly clear that all great artistes think alike and can rise above class and nation. The English artists agreed with Sisir Kumar Bhaduri on a great many points. For example, they were in accord as to the undesirability of an artiste appearing on both stage and screen. They felt that this would inevitably lead to a lowering of the acting standard in both these mediums. It should also be mentioned that while discussing the Bengali stage Sisir Kumar would frequently bring in analogies and comparisons with the British stage, Sybil Thorndike was so greatly impressed by his intimate knowledge of British stage traditions that she was heard to remark: 'It's really amazing, Mr Bhaduri, that you should be so well versed in matters connected with the English stage from ancient times right down to the present, whereas I know so little about your Bengali stage.'

She was not aware of the fact that besides being an actor of outstanding ability Sisir Kumar Bhaduri had also, through his studies, made himself thoroughly familiar with stage traditions both of this country as also of numerous foreign countries as well. Sir Lewis and Sybil Thorndike also repeatedly urged on Sisir Kumar Bhaduri that an actor of his standard and ability should unquestionably undertake a professional tour of England. After talking with them like old friends for a long time in that delightful atmosphere Sisir Kumar Bhaduri, before leaving, asked them to come and see one of his stage performances. For he would always assert and firmly believed that a stage artiste could not possibly be correctly assessed until he had been seen in a stage performance. The invitation was accepted with alacrity and on the appointed date Sir Lewis, Sybil Thorndike, etc., came to the Srirangam Theatre. The play performed that night was one written about the life of that outstanding Bengali poet of the 19th century, Michael Madhusudan Dutt. The visitors were entranced by the superb performance and their eyes never left the stage as scene succeeded scene. Dr Kalidas Nag was present to interpret the play to them, but Sybil Thorndike was heard to remark, 'No need of interpretation. Everything is crystal clear.' This will serve to emphasise how supremely successful the performance was that evening. During one of the intervals the author of this article showed Sybil Thorndike a picture of Michael Madhusudan which she eagerly studied and then, passing it on to Sir Lewis said : 'Look Lewis, what marvellous make up'.

As soon as the curtain had come down on the last scene they went up on to the stage to congratulate Sisir Kumar Bhaduri. The audience that night were privileged to witness a unique scene. Standing on each side of Sisir Kumar Bhaduri and holding his hands these distinguished English artistes expressed their heartfelt appreciation and gratitude. Time and again applause echoed throughout the theatre. Praising that night's magnificent performance Sybil Thorndike appealed to the audience to keep the theatre going. She also expressed the hope that a truly worthy theatre might be built to be directed by the great artiste Sisir Kumar Bhaduri. She averred that when she returned to London and wherever she went she would always express her admiration of Sisir Kumar Bhaduri's histrionic abilities. Sir Lewis then made a few remarks. He started by saying that nowhere else save on the Irish stage had he seen such free acting. He went on to declare that an actor of such outstanding stature as Sisir Kumar Bhaduri could quite easily gain fame all over the world, presenting his plays in his own language as the Russian actors were in the habit of doing.

In reply Sisir Kumar Bhaduri thanked them profusely for the praise they had bestowed on him. He also said that he was delighted that his performances had pleased them. He went on to add, however, that it was unfortunate that they had been denied the opportunity of seeing far greater Bengali actors than himself, such as Girish Chandra Ghose and others. He then said he would like them to know that the tradition of the Bengali stage went back a good five hundred years. This last statement was further proof to all his compatriots that Sisir Kumar Bhaduri was far more concerned with asserting the greatness of the Bengali stage rather than seeking glory for himself.

Sisir Kumar Bhaduri was a many faceted genius and it would be wrong to regard him merely as a great stage actor. He was extremely well read and very well versed in the art, literature, and history etc., both of his own country as also of many foreign countries as well. As regards his own particular sphere, the stage, he had at his fingertips all relevant matters regarding its history, traditions etc., and this knowledge was not confined to matters concerning the Bengali stage only. He was thoroughly familiar with the history and tradition of stages of numerous European countries and of America as well, and kept abreast of all developments connected with the dramatic art of these countries. It is not surprising therefore that when Paul Elliot Green the celebrated American dramatist, who won the Pulitzer Prize in 1927 for his play, *Abraham's Bosom*, met Sisir Kumar Bhaduri and described him as an inspiring personality.

It was during his tour of various European and Asian countries under a Rockefeller Foundation grant, to study dramatic and dance art of different countries, while passing through Calcutta he met Sisir Kumar Bhaduri. He discussed with Bhaduri various matters connected with the Bengali stage and its probable future and was deeply struck by our great actor's profound knowledge and impressive personality. A paper remarked:

> 'Mr. Green said after the meeting that he was highly impressed by the 'inspiring personality' of Mr. Sisir Kumar Bhaduri and thought 'he symbolizes the hope of future India.'" (*American Reporter*, 12th Dec. 1951).'

Yet one more incident may here be related concerning the deep impression his acting and personality made on another *famous American dramatic critic*. Sisir Kumar Bhaduri's theatre Srirangam was closed at the time. He was then appearing on the stage of the Minerva Theatre in a play called *Jibanranga*. A foreign lady asked for an interview with him one evening after a performance and was shown into his dressing room. She first said that shortly before leaving Delhi for Calcutta she had been informed by a friend that Sisir Kumar Bhaduri would be performing for just a few days at the Minerva Theatre and that she should on no account miss the opportunity of seeing him. She went on to declare that she would indeed have been deprived of the privilege of seeing an outstanding stage performance had she not come that evening. She also admitted that she had never before known that acting of such a high order was to be seen here, nor that there were artistes of Sisir Kumar Bhaduri's stature. Sisir Kumar Bhaduri thanked her profusely and then asked if he might know her name. She replied that she was Rosamond Gilder. Immediately Sisir

Kumar Bhaduri made a reference to a certain American stage magazine and remarked that she must be connected with it as he had seen her name mentioned there. The lady was truly amazed that he should be so well informed in matters connected with the American stage, and inquired how this came about. Smilingly Sisir Kumar Bhaduri responded that they were both inhabitants of *One World*. Declaring that she was leaving for home the very next day but would certainly come back sometime to see him again in a number of plays, Rosamond Gilder shook him warmly by the hand and departed.

Unfortunately they were not destined to meet again but so deep an impression did Sisir Kumar Bhaduri made on Rosamond Gilder by that one performance of his that she witnessed that she could never forget him thereafter. On her return to the States she would regularly send him each month complimentary copies of *Theatre Art*. She also sent him as a present through the U.S.I.S. a copy of her book *Introduction to the Theatre*. The letter sent by the U.S.I.S. along with this book so adequately expresses the high regard that Rosamond Gilder must have had for Sisir Kumar Bhaduri that it will be quite appropriate to quote the same here. They wrote:

U.S.I.S.
7, Chowringhee Road
Calcutta – 13
January 16, 1957
Mr. Sisir Kumar Bhaduri
238, Barrackpore Trunk Road, Calcutta – 35.

Dear Mr. Bhaduri,

During the recent visit of Dr Rosamond Gilder, Director of the United States Centre of the International Theatre Institute, we visited your theatre and had the great pleasure of meeting you. I recently had a letter from Miss. Gilder in which she sent her greetings to you.

The United States Service has just received one copy of an *Introduction to the Theatre*. It seems to me that no one in Calcutta could be more interested in the subject than you, and so we send it to you with our compliments.

With all best wishes,
Sincerely,
For the Public Affairs Officer.
Sd/- Aileen Aderton
Cultural Affairs Officer.

An attempt has here been made to record some of the achievements of that outstanding personality born in Bengal who through his unique genius earned for the Bengali stage the respect and admiration of gifted and distinguished people of various nations.

It was aptly remarked by Saumyendra Nath Tagore, at Sisir Kumar Bhaduri's first death anniversary on the 30th June last, that he had proved a worthy successor of Rabindranath Tagore.

First published as '*Sisir Kumar in the Eyes of Foreigners*' in *Puja Annual, Hindustan Standard*, 1960

RABINDRANATH TAGORE AND SISIR KUMAR BHADURI

RABINDRANATH TAGORE AND SISIR KUMAR BHADURI

It was while discussing the role of music in the learning and culture of our nation that Rabindranath once remarked –

> 'Only the other day our Nataraj Sisir Bhaduri demanded some songs from me suitable for a certain stately and tragic play.'

Sisir Kumar Bhaduri, who was fortunate enough to be thus described as '*Nataraj*' by the poet who, by any reckoning was among the foremost actors, dramatists and critics the world has ever known, made his first stage appearance in the poet's presence while still a student.

One of the events celebrating Rabindranath's fiftieth birthday was a performance of *Baikunther Khata* put on by members of the Calcutta University Institute. Sisir Kumar Bhaduri, then an active and popular member of the Institute, took the part of Kedar in the play. So delighted was the poet at the excellent performance put on that occasion that he spoke highly of it in one of his letters to Amal Home. In this letters (dated 23rd Magh 1318 BS) he asked Amal Home to tell his friends at the Institute how much he enjoyed their performance. He also expressed the view that barring members of his own household such as Gaganendranath and Abanindranath, no one could have staged so distinguished a production of this particular play. He confessed that he envied the actor who had played the part of Kedar as he himself was once celebrated in that role.

In this connection it should be borne in mind that Sisir Kumar Bhaduri, then an amateur, had not yet met the poet and that the praise he earned from Rabindranath the very first time he performed before him was entirely on his merit as an actor.

Some ten years later Sisir Kumar Bhaduri gave up his post as a professor and devoted himself to the professional stage. By this time he had come to know the poet quite well. Within a short time he was able to set up his own theatre, the Natyamandir. It was at this theatre that, on the 6th of August 1924, the first performance of *Sita* was staged on a most elaborate scale in the presence of such distinguished members of the audience as Rasaraj Amritlal Bose, Deshbandhu Chittaranjan Das and scores of other prominent citizens. The acting, the stage settings and the costumes were all of such unparalleled excellence that the fame of that supremely successful performance spread throughout the land almost overnight. It was not long before Rabindranath too came to hear about this play and visited the theatre to see it shortly after its opening. Writing about the poet's visit to the theatre, a Bengali weekly paper remarked that it was certainly a memorable day for the *Manmohon*-Natyamandir as it had the privilege of welcoming among the audience, who came to see the performance of *Sita*, the greatest poet of the present age. Referring to the distinguished audience present on the occasion the paper goes on to say –

> 'At no other Bengali theatre have we ever before seen so vast an array of litterateurs and connoisseurs of the stage as were present at the *Manmohon - Natyamandir* last Sunday. This establishes beyond question that, among connoisseurs, no other actor can now even approach Sisir Kumar in celebrity.' (*Nautchghar*, 6th Bhadra 1331 BS).

A good deal developed, however, from Rabindranath's attendance at the performance of *Sita* that evening. While there was naturally general rejoicing at the emergence of a new stage star, the event was the cause of a good deal of disquiet and apprehension at another celebrated Calcutta theatre of the time. The group connected with this theatre realized only too well that it would be beyond their capacity or that of anyone else for that matter to compete with such outstanding genius as Sisir Kumar Bhaduri. Left with no other recourse, they embarked on a press campaign to depreciate Sisir Kumar Bhaduri and his company in the eyes of the theatre-going public.

At the same time a pamphlet, couched in indecent language, was issued which was distributed free of charge among the citizens. In this, fun was poked at the performance of *Sita* and Sisir Kumar Bhaduri's entire company, who had earned such high praise from Rabindranath and scores of other distinguished critics. In spite of their adverse propaganda, *Sita* continued to play to packed houses every night, a good many people even being turned away disappointed since no more tickets were available. At this the opposite party grew desperate and resorted to a most contemptible device. Through the papers they had the report spread that Rabindranath had not liked the performance a bit. Both the general run of theatre goers as also the poet himself were amazed and distressed at this unfounded report. In a letter (dated 12th Bhadra 1331 BS) to the well-known litterateur Manilal Ganguli, Rabindranath protested against this spurious complaint. In this letter he said that it was hardly possible for him to write about the play in the papers himself. He, therefore, suggested that Manilal Ganguli should be good enough to write to the papers and say that he (Rabindranath) had the very highest opinion of Sisir Kumar Bhaduri's qualities as a producer, so much so that he had of his own accord entrusted Sisir Kumar Bhaduri with the staging of some of his own plays.

He went on to say that he had not particularly liked the drama *Sita*. He felt he could hardly describe it as a play at all and it provided little scope for acting excellence. Nevertheless, he said, Sisir Kumar Bhaduri had exerted his superb directorial skill towards making this a stage success. He said that Manilal Ganguli could quote him as having expressed these opinions.

Manilal Ganguli quoted from this letter in one of his own which he had published in *Nautchghar* (20th Bhadra 1331 BS) as a protest against the false report put out. In this letter he said –

> 'Efforts are being made to circulate a rumour in the city to the effect that Rabindranath ran down the performance of Sita staged at the Manmohon-Natyamandir.
>
> This rumour is totally unfounded. I know for a fact that Rabindranath did not disparage the performance in any way and can therefore send off this letter of protest with the fullest assurance. .....As it happens, I was with Rabindranath the night he attended the performance and stayed with him right up to the end of the play. During the intervals he discussed the play with me at considerable length.....
>
> The moment I heard the report that Rabindranath had allegedly spoken slightingly of the play, I asked him straight out if this were actually the case. He stoutly denied ever having said a depreciatory word about it to anyone. On the contrary, he declared, he had spoken highly of the production to all who had asked him his opinion in this regard. Parts of the play had impressed him most favourably, as he told me himself the night we saw the performance together. Moreover, he had no hesitation in pronouncing the scenery, stage-settings, music and dancing as of a high order.

Rabindranath considers it a most encouraging sign for the dramatic art of the nation that Sisir Kumar should be exerting himself in the laudable endeavour of raising the standard of the Bengali stage. He was particularly curious to see what Sisir Kumar had made of the play *Sita* and it was to satisfy his curiosity in this regard that he went to the *Manmohon-Natyamandir* that evening, although normally, as I well know, he seldom attends Bengali plays. It is quite obvious that Sisir Kumar has succeeded in impressing Rabindranath most favourably in regard to his capacities as a producer so much so that the poet felt impelled to invite Sisir Kumar to his house to give him the benefit of his advice and suggestions and to discuss with him various aspects of acting and the dramatic art. The poet had no desire to confine the discussions to a detailed analysis of the merits and demerits of the play *Sita*. The success achieved by Sisir Kumar could be given no higher certificate than the earnest desire it had inspired in the poet to devote all the care he could to help in determining the course of this most talented actor's professional career.......'

It was earnestly hoped that the publication of this letter would mark the end of this unpleasant incident but unfortunately this was not to be. Sisir Kumar Bhaduri's opponents put out hints that the letter of Rabindranath's quoted by Manilal Ganguli was spurious. They even went so far as to try to vent their spleen on the poet himself, and published a cartoon of him in their paper.

Nautchghar was to take a more decisive action within a few days. It announced in its columns that it was prepared to pay a cash reward to anyone who could prove as spurious the letter of Rabindranath's from which an extract had been quoted. The announcement reads as follows –

'We shall pay a thousand rupees in cash to anyone who is able to secure from Rabindranath a denial of the authenticity of the letter from him quoted in our columns by Manilal Babu.'

It seems hardly necessary to state that this challenge evoked no response from anyone as it was obviously impossible for *Nautchghar*'s offer to be taken up.

The poet, however, was still not entirely free of doubt and suspicion in this regard. He was at that time about to undertake a voyage abroad and was apprehensive that advantage might be taken of his absence from India for the dissemination of fresh malign rumours. Before leaving the country, therefore, he wrote another letter to Manilal Ganguli. In this letter he asked Manilal Ganguli to take suitable steps, should circumstances develop along these lines, as he feared they might, during his absence. He entrusted Manilal Ganguli with the responsibility of scotching any such rumours if they should be started.

As it happened, however, no steps on these lines proved to be of any necessity.

It should be mentioned in this connection that though the acting in *Sita* had impressed the poet most favourably, the play itself had not been to his liking, as was clear from his letter to Manilal Ganguli. Rabindranath therefore thought of writing a play based on the *Mahabharat* for Sisir Kumar Bhaduri, but somehow this was never accomplished, but Manilal Ganguli's letter establishes beyond question that Rabindranath entrusted Sisir Kumar Bhaduri with the staging of some of his plays. References to this fact are to be found in issues of *Nautchghar* of that period. The paper states that Rabindranath effected a number of changes in his *Chirakumar Shabha* so as to render it more stageworthy for Sisir Kumar Bhaduri. It had previously been half-novel and half-play, but he converted it into a full-fledged play.

The undernoted item appears in another issue of the same paper and it says –

> 'Shortly before undertaking his present foreign trip Rabindranath sent for Streejukta Sisir Kumar Bhaduri, the leading actor in Bengal today, and read out to him his play *Rakta-Karabi*. We understand that Sisir Kumar expressed a keen desire to stage this play. What has happened about the staging of this play?'

It is really most surprising that though a number of Rabindranath's plays were put on, the above two plays were never produced at Bhaduri's theatre. True, Sisir Kumar Bhaduri himself more than once played the roles of Chandra Babu or Rasik in *Chirakumar Sabha*, but these were in performances staged at the Art Theatre and not at the Natyamandir.

Sesh-Raksha was put on with great éclat at the Natyamandir in the year 1927. An amusing incident in this connection seems worth relating. It was at Sisir Kumar Bhaduri's request that the poet made certain alterations in his story *Goray Galad* to produce a revised play, *Sesh-Raksha*. When the new work was completed, Rabindranath sent for Sisir Kumar Bhaduri and handed the completed manuscript to him. Observing that the name too had been changed Sisir Kumar Bhaduri ventured to remark '*Gurudev, the name Goray Galad is one that would have proved attractive to theatregoers.*' A flicker of amusement lit the poet's expressive eyes for a moment and then in a grave and affectedly disappointed tone he replied, '*Goray galad chhilo kete kute sesh raksha korlam, tao tomar mon pelamna, Sisir!*' (There were initial mistakes and I made a lot of alternations as a last saving device, but I still don't seem to have been able to satisfy you, Sisir).

To revert to the performance of this comedy at the Natyamandir, it would be appropriate to stress the fact that the pre-eminent producer spared no pains to ensure that the production should be an unqualified success. Dinendrnath Tagore was entrusted with the task of training the cast in the songs included in the play. In this connection it may be mentioned that on each occasion when Sisir Kumar Bhaduri staged one of Rabindranath's plays, for training in regard to the songs in the play, he would invariably rely on either Dinendranath Tagore or Anadi Kumar Dastidar, both life-long devotees of the songs of Tagore and pre-eminent authorities in the regard.

The play soon became a great success and Rabindranath came to the theatre one evening to see the performance, which pleased him immensely. It was the last scene that he found most attractive. In this scene a novelty was introduced by Sisir Kumar Bhaduri in the form of the abolition of distinction between stage and auditorium. Though this unity of action of theatrical intimacy was in vogue in Europe at that time, it was Sisir Kumar Bhaduri who first introduced it to this country. In the course of this scene Sisir Kumar Bhaduri and other artistes came down from the stage and conversed freely with the members of the audience, whom they invited to Gadai Chandra's wedding reception. A number of people were at first startled almost out of their wits by this striking innovation, but later a good many of them accepted the invitation and came up on the stage to join the actors at Gadai Chandra's wedding reception. It should also be remarked that some of the members of the audience joined in the last song. The poet greatly enjoyed this new departure in the presentation of the play.

In September 1927 Sisir Kumar Bhaduri staged *Bisarjan*. He took the utmost pains to ensure that not the acting alone but every single aspect of the production should be of such a high order as to ensure a successful performance. Dinendranath Tagore was music director for the performance. Ramendranath Chatterjee, a skilled stage decorator whose work was admired even by Abanindranath, undertook the painting of the scenes. The producer also paid careful attention to the costumes. He availed himself of the advice and instructions of Tripura's Barathakur to ensure authenticity, in regard to cut, colour and manner of wearing, of the costumes to be worn by the members of Tripura's royal family. The audiences of the day were in fact privileged to see a play of Tagore's presented in the best possible manner.

Rabindranath also put on this play a number of times and would act in it himself either in the role of Jai Singha or in that of Raghupati. Sisir Kumar Bhaduri too, on several occasions, had played one or other of these roles himself. His flawless acting in the part of Jai Singha would hold the audiences spell-bound, but the unparalleled excellence of his rendering of the role of Raghupati positively amazed the onlookers, leaving on their minds an impression that time could never erase. The distinguished stage critic Hemendra Kumar Roy once confessed to the author of this article that he found so little to choose between the supreme renderings of the role of Raghupati by both Rabindranath and Sisir Kumar Bhaduri that he had not been able to make up his mind as to which of them was better in the part. Sisir Kumar Bhaduri's performance of *Bisarjan* delighted the poet himself as also the audience that thronged the theatre to see it.

The poet also visited Sisir Kumar Bhaduri's theatre to see a performance of his play *Tapati*. It might be appropriate to mention that it is still not generally known that some well-wishers of Sisir Kumar Bhaduri strongly urged him not to stage this play. They felt that bulk of the theatre goers would not be able to appreciate so refined a play and that in consequence Sisir Kumar Bhaduri might be involved in a heavy loss on the production. This argument carried little weight with Sisir Kumar Bhaduri who, all his life, was an unfaltering devotee of the dramatic art. He would constantly express his firm belief that the theatre's most nobling purpose was to educate the theatre-going public in such a way that they could gain an appreciation of good plays and good acting. His friend's warning, therefore, went unheeded and *Tapati* was put on at great expense.

Only a few months earlier this play had been staged at the poet's house at Jorasanko for four nights in succession. The poet himself had taken the part of Vikramdev, the king of Jalandhar. A paper of that period reports, however, that before it was put on at the Natyamandir the poet made a number of alterations in the play, the better to adapt it for presentation at a public theatre. It should be mentioned that Sisir Kumar Bhaduri preserved the revised manuscript of *Tapati* with the utmost care throughout his life, regarding it as one of his most treasured possessions.

The play duly opened at the appointed date. Sisir Kumar Bhaduri himself took the part of Vikramdev. The roles of Naresh and Ratneswar were played by Jiban Ganguli and Rabi Roy respectively. Jogesh Chowdhuri appeared in Devdatta's role. The female parts of Rani Sumitra and Bipasha were played by the doyen actresses Prabha and Kankabati respectively.

The highly successful performance was reviewed at great length by *Nautchghar* in its issue of 3rd Magh 1336 BS. Its dramatic critic starts off by saying that Sisir Kumar Bhaduri's interpretation of the role of Vikramadev showed no sign of having been influenced by Rabindranath's rendering of the part. His distinctive rendering of the role of Vikramdev was indeed worthy of Sisir Kumar Bhaduri. It is neither possible nor in fact necessary to quote in extensive from the lengthy review. It is sufficient to say that in the critic's opinion the incomparable artist gave a superb rendering of the regally arrogant and imperious character of Vikramdev. His silent acting in the Martanda Temple in the last scene positively enthralled the audience.

Though very busy at the time Rabindranath accepted the invitation extended to him to come and see the performance. He followed the play with close attention throughout. His presence in the auditorium that evening seemed to inspire the cast to even greater efforts. When the curtain came down and it was time for him to leave, the poet, who had been highly impressed by the most entrancing performance, conveyed his hearty and sincere congratulations to Sisir Kumar Bhaduri.

In spite of the faultless acting and the praise it had earned from Rabindranath, the play did not have a successful run. The warnings uttered by Sisir Kumar Bhaduri's friends before he put on the production proved to be accurate prophecies indeed. After the first few performances audience attendance began to dwindle. After only thirteen shows Sisir Kumar Bhaduri was not merely obliged to take off the play but even compelled to close down his theatre.

Later the poet came to see his social drama *Jogajog* at the *Naba-Natyamandir* set up by Sisir Kumar Bhaduri. It will be an adequate appreciation of this play to quote Rabindranath in this regard, who said of it –

> 'I was rather doubtful in mind when I accepted the invitation to see *Jogajog* at the *Nava-Natyamandir*. I returned from the performance, however, both delighted and amazed. One rarely sees a play so competently acted. If in spite of this it does not

> catch on with the public, no blame can attach to Natyadhinayak Sreejukta Sisir Bhaduri.'

Rabindranath came to see yet another play *Ritimata Natak* produced by Sisir Kumar Bhaduri. Some people tried to dissuade him from going to see this play, written by Sisir Kumar Bhaduri and Jaladhar Chatterjee. In this context it would perhaps be appropriate to quote the description of this amusing incident by Charu Chandra Bhattacharya, who was for many years a colleague of the poet's and a true connoisseur of the dramatic art. He says –

> 'Rabindranath has seen a great many of his own plays performed at public theatres and has lavished praise on certain actors and actresses. But he had a special affection for Sisir Kumar. In this connection I should like to dwell on a particular incident. When the play *Ritimata Natak* was on at his theatre Sisir Kumar called on Rabindranath to invite him to the performance, and this invitiation was accepted by the poet. After Sisir Kumar had left some of the people who were with Rabindranath tried to dissuade him from seeing this play, urging that it would hardly be worth his while to see a play written by someone else. Rabindranath replied, '*Sisir would be deeply hurt if I refuse to go*'. Sisir Babu came to call for him that evening and he went with him to see the performance……'

It might be remarked that on that occasion too the poet thoroughly enjoyed the excellent acting and highly skilful direction.

I shall conclude this article by relating an incident illustrative of the high regard in which the Kaviguru was held by Sisir Kumar Bhaduri. Once, in the course of a discussion the present writer was having with Sisir Kumar Bhaduri on the subject of the Bengali stage the matter suddenly cropped up of foreigners coming to see him act. At this Sisir Kumar Bhaduri suddenly grew restless and excited. He exclaimed,

'Far from feeling any satisfaction at praise lavished on me by foreigners who have seen my performance, and who have remarked that they had certainly not expected to see acting of such a high order here, I feel annoyed and resentful. Do they imagine that it is only on their own fertile soil that artistes can grow, and that our barren and unproductive land can bear no great artistes?'

The next moment he regained his composure. Gazing at the star-spangled dark expanse of the night sky he went on to say, as though to himself, '*They seem to forget that this is the land of Tagore.*'

First published as *'Rabindranath and Sisir Kumar'* in *Puja Annual, Hindustan Standard*, 1964

SISIR KUMAR BHADURI
IN
SARAT CHANDRA CHATTERJEE'S PLAYS

SISIR KUMAR BHADURI IN SARAT CHANDRA CHATTERJEE'S PLAYS

Sarat Chandra once wrote in 25th Aswin 1341 BS to the then joint editor of *Nautchghar*.

> 'Who is to perform any plays I might write? Where are the educated and discerning actors and actresses to be found? I have yet to come across an actress worthy of filling the role of a heroine in a play.'

Sisir Kumar Bhaduri, that actor without peer, repeatedly gave the lie to these baseless and unjustified statements of Sarat Chandra. He staged a great many of Sarat Chandra's plays and in almost all cases the productions were outstandingly successful.

It would here be appropriate to mention that Sisir Kumar Bhaduri appeared in the very first film version of one of Sarat Chandra's books *Andhare Alo*, that was in the days of the silent film. The picture was graced by another outstanding actor Naresh Chandra Mitra.

A play of Sarat Chandra's was first staged at Sisir Kumar Bhaduri's theatre Natyamandir in 1927, a time when the playhouse was at the height of its glory. Any plays put on there were assured of instant success and would regularly draw crowded houses night after night. A notice appeared to the effect that *Sorosi* was to be staged at the Natyamandir on the 6th of August. Predictably, reaction to this announcement was most favourable and theatre-goers eagerly awaited the opportunity of seeing the outstanding actor of their day Sisir Kumar Bhaduri and his distinguished company in a play by Sarat Chandra.

Sorosi opened on the very appointed day. Sisir Bhaduri himself appeared in the role of Jibananda. The parts of Ekkari, Janardan, Shiromoni, Sagar Sardar and Nirmal were played respectively by Gopaldas Bhattacharya, Jogesh Chowdhuri, Amalendu Lahiri, Monoranjan Bhattacharya and Sailen Chowdhuri. The talented actress Charusila appeared in the title role.

In common with other plays which Bhaduri directed and in which he took part himself, *Sorosi* was an immediate success. Reproduced below is the gist of what the weekly paper of that period *Nautchghar* (27th Sravan 1334 BS) had to say about the play, as this will make abundantly clear what an outstanding hit it must have been. Of Sisir Kumar Bhaduri's memorable performance as Jibananda they remark –

> 'Sisir Kumar in his performance in the role of Jibananda has set up a shining example of what unimaginable beauty can be lent to a truly great play by the inimitable talent of a born actor.'

They also had this to say of the distinguished actor's performance –

> 'This rendering adds a new dimension to the character that Saratchandra has created, We are convinced that the playwright himself will be overwhelmed by the performance, for Sisir Kumar has conceivably carried the writer's imaginative purpose a stage further..... It is in the role of Jibananda that we have observed the supreme flowering of Sisir Kumar's dramatic power and skill.'

Of Charusila's flawless rendering of the title role, the dramatic critic of *Nautchghar* said the actress had rendered her extremely difficult role with such supreme skill that he simply could not find words of praise adequate to her distinguished performance. He also expressed the view that so high a standard of acting would be a matter of pride for any top-ranking actress of the past or present.

He also praises the performances of the artistes in the other roles and has complimentary things to say about the scenes painted by Ramendranath Chattopadhya, a student of Abanindranath.

It was only natural that performances of such all-round excellence of a distinguished play like *Sorosi* should draw crowded houses, night after night. The play had long run and we learn from the papers of the period that a number of erudite theatre-goers saw it more than once. It is, for example, reported in *Nautchghar* of the 16th Bhadra 1334 BS that the well-known poet Narendra Dev had announced his intention of seeing the play sixteen nights in succession and had adhered to his resolve. Many others would also come to the theatre again and again to see the play. This is not a bit surprising as these performances of *Sorosi* offered the combined attractions of Saratchandra's outstanding talent as a dramatist and Sisir Kumar Bhaduri's unrivalled histrionic skill.

The now well-known and popular play of Sarat Chandra's *Palli Samaj* was first staged in 1928 at another renowned theatre of the period—the Art Theatre. The performance here proved a failure, however, and the play was taken off after just a few days. The rumour spread that it was not faulty acting but weaknesses in the play itself that proved responsible for this unsuccessful run. The dramatist, when he heard this, was most hurt and aggrieved; he therefore earnestly requested Sisir Kumar Bhaduri to stage this play to prove to audiences that it was not the fault of the playwright that the performance at the Art Theatre had been such a flop. Sisir Kumar Bhaduri was most reluctant to stage a play that had so recently failed at another theatre but found it hard to resist Sarat Chandra's importunity. At Sisir Kumar Bhaduri's suggestion, however, the playwright made certain changes in the play and renamed it *Rama*.

It was in 1929 that it was staged at the Natyamandir. Sisir Kumar Bhaduri himself took the role of Ramesh. The title role was played by that talented actress Prova. Artistes such as Jogesh Chowdhuri, Amalendu Lahiri etc. filled the other roles in the play. Sisir Kumar Bhaduri, that great director, made an outstanding success of the play that had recently failed at another theatre. A dramatic critic who saw the show expressed the opinion that the performance of *Rama* at the Natyamandir was far superior to that which had been staged at the Art Theatre, the audience had been overwhelmed by Sisir Kumar Bhaduri's masterly rendering of the role of Ramesh, and he felt that Prova, in the title role, had played her part to perfection. It might here be remarked that after this successful stage performance, New Theatres persuaded Sisir Kumar Bhaduri and his company to do the film version of *Palli Samaj*.

It is worth mentioning that Sisir Kumar Bhaduri would from time to time play the roles of Beni or Gobinda, thus demonstrating to audiences that a gifted actor can make such of even a minor role and need not necessarily be cast in the leading role.

Sarat Chandra's play *Birajbau* was staged at Sisir Kumar's theatre *Naba* Natyamandir on the 28th of July 1934. Sisir Kumar Bhaduri took the part of Nilamba, an ignorant, headstrong character addicted to drugs and yet, at the same time a simple, rustic type. His masterly rendering of the role entranced his vast audiences. The rising actress Kankabati who took the part of Biraj put up a very good performance. It is appropriate to mention that Sisir Kumar

Bhaduri donated the entire box office takings on the opening night to Mahatma Gandhi's Harijan fund.

Another play of the popular dramatist opened at Sisir Kumar Bhaduri's theatre on the 22nd December 1934. This was *Bijoya.* Sisir Kumar Bhaduri took the part of Rashbehari. That skilled and handsome actor Biswanath Bhaduri played the role of Naren. The parts of Dayal, Nalini and Bilash were played respectively by Sital Paul, Ranibala and Sailen Chowdhuri. The beautiful actress Kankabati was in the title role.

As in the case of *Sorosi*, *Bijoya* too proved an instant hit and drew packed houses night after night. Sisir Kumar Bhaduri's skilful direction built up a faultless and enchanting production. Kankabati put on such a magnificent performance in the title role that the dramatic critic of *Nautchghar*, in his review appearing in that Journal of the 12th Pous 1341 BS was compelled to admit that at times her brilliance put even Sisir Kumar Bhaduri's finished rendering of the character of Rashbehari in the shade. He had no hesitation in asserting that this was the finest role Kankabati had ever played since the start of her stage career. He concluded with the phrase — 'She has said the last word in acting.' The reviewer was likewise favourably impressed with Biswanath's masterly portrayal of the character of Naren. He praised him lavishly as also Sailen Chowdhuri in the part of Bilash.

The critic states that every single member of the audience thoroughly enjoyed Sisir Kumar Bhaduri's performance. He goes on to say that by swift adjustment of his expression and tone of voice to suit different occurrences and altering circumstances and by adroit stroking of his beard from time to time, he was able to make crystal clear to the audience the different phases of character of the hypocritical yet powerful Rashbehari, skilled in diplomacy.

The play *Achala* started its run round about the puja season of 1936. *Achala* was the stage version of that much praised as also much slated book of Sarat Chandra's named *Grihadaha*. It might here be mentioned that whereas books are normally staged before they are filmed, *Grihadaha* had already been filmed before the stage version was put up.

In the play, Sisir Kumar Bhaduri played the role of Kedar Babu, Achala's father. It is quite a minor role given an actor but little scope and yet, through his supreme histrionic skill Sisir Kumar Bhaduri transformed it into a vital role. The audience were amazed at this seeming miracle. Biswanath, Sisir Kumar Bhaduri's able and worthy brother, played the part of Suresh. He had played the same role in the film version. His stage performance was much more natural and impressive, however, and earned him generous praise in the press (*Chhanda*, 11th Agrahayan 1343 BS). It is worth recording that on some nights Sisir Kumar Bhaduri himself played the part of Suresh on the stage. The critic also praised the artistes who played the parts of Achala, Mahim and Mrinal.

Bhaduri also staged two other popular works of Sarat Chandra at his theatre *Sree Rangam*. One was *Bipradas* and the other *Bindur Chheley*. Many people were firmly convinced that unless Sisir Kumar Bhaduri himself took part in the performance no play put on at his theatre could possibly succeed. This illusion was effectively destroyed in 1943 and 1944 with the staging of the above two plays, in which Sisir Kumar Bhaduri did not at first appear himself but confined his activities to the direction of the performance. Under the guidance of the greatest director of the modern Bengali stage, distinguished artistes such as Biswanath Bhaduri, Prova, Nivanani, Molina, Ranjit Roy and others put on such a tasteful and unblemished performance that both plays ran a long while, drawing packed houses. Long after the opening Sisir Kumar Bhaduri appeared in the title role of *Bipradas* and in the part of Jadab in *Bindur Chheley*.

The article may fittingly be concluded with a piece of information that will probably be news to many. In a discussion with the present writer regarding Sarat Chandra's plays Sisir Kumar Bhaduri once confided that he had long cherished a desire to stage Sarat Chandra's highly controversial work *Shesh Prashna*. He would have liked to play the part of Ashu Babu himself. When asked why he had not been able in pulling it off he replied with a curry smile – 'There were a lot of obstacles, but the one was to find an actress capable of portraying the role of Kamal.'

First published as '*Sisir Bhaduri in Saratchandra's Plays*', *The Sunday Hindustan Standard*. 24.04.1966

SISIR KUMAR BHADURI IN GIRISH CHANDRA GHOSH'S PLAYS

SISIR KUMAR BHADURI IN GIRISH CHANDRA GHOSH'S PLAYS

A schoolboy, once with Charu Chandra Gupta—son of Mahendra Nath Gupta, the compiler of '*The Gospel of Sri Ramakrishna*'—presented himself before Girish Chandra.

This boy had entered a school recitation competition and his object in visiting the great Girish Chandra was to get some sort of training or instruction about the recitation. The boy recited a passage from Michael Madhusudan's *Meghnad Badh Kavya*. Girish Chandra listened to his recitation, corrected the youngster slightly in just one or two parts and remarked he was confident that the boy would win the competition and, sure enough, this schoolboy did win the first place.

The handsome boy was none other than Sisir Kumar Bhaduri, who was later to become the initiator of a new era in the Bengali stage. This was the first occasion on which he met Girish Chandra. The latter could scarcely have imagined that his young visitor was destined to transform the Bengali stage and revolutionise the manner of acting, the stage settings and costumes. What is more, he could never in the wildest dreams have thought that this schoolboy visitor of his would later stage some of his (Girish Chandra's) plays and portray his most difficult roles, those that the author himself would often fail, with such consummate skill as to hold vast audiences spellbound night after night.

During his early amateur days, when he was connected with the Calcutta University Institute and the renowned Old Club of Bowbazar and later on the professional stage, Sisir Kumar Bhaduri acted in a number of Girish Chandra's plays such as *Jana*, *Buddhadev*, *Pandaver Agnyatabas*, *Asoke*, *Balidan*, *Prafulla*, *Bilwamangal*, *Pandav Gourav*, *Dakshya Jagna*. It will not be possible in this brief article to do more than just list the roles in which he appeared while an amateur, in Girish Chandra's plays.

Buddhadev was staged at Calcutta University in September, 1910, Sisir Kumar Bhaduri appearing in the title role. Naresh Chandra Mitra, the well-known and popular actor, also appeared in this performance.

Then again in 1912 an elaborate performance of Girish Chandra's evergreen play *Jana* was put on at the Calcutta University Institute. Sisir Kumar Bhaduri played the role of Prabir. Kanti Chandra Mukherjee appeared in the title role. Sir Gooroodas Banerjee, Sir Asutosh Mukherjee and a number of other distinguished people were present at this outstandingly successful performance. At the conclusion Sir Gooroodas Banerjee, Sir Asutosh Mukherjee, the eminent lawyer Mr N.K. Basu, Prof Khagendra Nath Mitra and others announced their intention of presenting medals to Sisir Kumar Bhaduri and certain others who had taken part in the performance as a mark of recognition of the histrionic skill they had displayed.

Hastily consulting the other artistes who had been promised medals, however, Sisir Kumar Bhaduri expressed his deepest gratitude to their patrons but said it would give the cast far greater pleasure if the money, instead of being spent on medals, were donated to the students' fund of the Institute. It is quite obvious that it was Sisir Kumar Bhaduri who had induced his fellow artistes to forfeit the medals they had earned.

And he, while still a student, displayed such utter indifference to the glamour of medals and other rewards and found no difficulty in later life in being supremely indifferent to Government titles, which is not in the least surprising.

Then in September 1913, the members of the CUI staged Girish Chandra's *Ashoke.* Sisir Kumar Bhaduri appeared in the title role. Other roles were filled by Naresh Mitra, Kanti Mukherjee, Nagendra Bose, Raghabendra Banerjee, Kalika Mitra, Biswanath Bhaduri etc. In common with other plays staged at the CUI this was an outstanding success.

At a performance of *Pandaver Agnyatabas* staged at the Old Club Sisir Kumar Bhaduri played the roles of Bhim and the aged Brahmin, lending distinction to both these parts through his excellent acting. This was his last stage appearance as an amateur. He had also produced and directed the play. The distinguished dramatic critic Hemendra Kumar Roy who had attended this performance wrote a lengthy review of this performance in the well-known paper of the day, *Hindusthan*, most of which was devoted to praise of Sisir Kumar Bhaduri, whose skill as producer was likewise commended by the critic. This was the first occasion on which a stage performance of Sisir Kumar Bhaduri was mentioned in a press review. It may be mentioned here that up to that time Hemendra Kumar Roy had not even met Sisir Kumar Bhaduri though later they were to become fast friends.

On the professional stage Sisir Kumar Bhaduri appeared in the leading roles of such plays by Girish Chandra as *Jana*, *Prafulla*, *Bilwamangal*, *Balidan*, *Ashoke*, *Pandaver Agnyatabas*, *Pandav Gourav*, *Dakshya Jagnya*, *Buddhadev*, *Sirajudaulla* etc.

On the professional stage Sisir Kumar Bhaduri's first appearance in a play of Girish Chandra's was in the ever-popular

Jana. It is well worth recording that before the performance Sisir Kumar Bhaduri had made certain changes in the play to make it more forceful to contemporary audiences. Certain scenes and portions of dialogues had been omitted to better present the play's true essence. The costumes, scenes and dances were all designed to attract the interest of the people of the modern age (*Bangla Rangalaya O Sisir Kumar*). Sisir Kumar Bhaduri played the part of Prabir. Frequently filling this role while still an amateur he had had no difficulty in capturing the hearts of his audience and earning a great reputation by his incomparable rendering of the part. A few words about the performance of the actress who appeared in the title role would not be out of place here. At Sisir Kumar Bhaduri's request the part was played by Tarasundari, a renowned actress of an earlier period. She had virtually retired from the stage at the time of the performance, but Sisir Kumar Bhaduri's importunity induced her to take the part. The combined efforts of these two outstanding artistes of an old and new age resulted in an incredibly impressive and successful performance. To this day, those who were fortunate enough to see the play and are still among us have the most vivid recollection of a theatrical treat that is presented but rarely to an audience. The dramatic critic Hemendra Kumar Roy said that the actress had not taken any training from Sisir Kumar Bhaduri, but rendered the role as she thought. Even appearing with the greatest actor of the new era, however, her genius and greatness had at all times been apparent and she was able to maintain the supremacy of her role (*Jader Dekhechi*).

Sisir Kumar Bhaduri, from time to time, would also play other roles in *Jana*, such as those of Niladhaja and Bidushaka, amazing audiences by the diversity of his talent.

Another outstanding role in one of Girish Chandra's plays to be portrayed by Sisir Kumar Bhaduri was that of Jogesh in *Prafulla*. Besides Girish Chandra himself, such celebrated artistes of an earlier age such as Ardhendushekhar, Amarendranath and Dani Babu also took part in the role of Jogesh. Audiences had naturally been most eager to savour the portrayal of the difficult role of Jogesh by the star of the modern age.

On the opening night audiences were immediately struck by Sisir Kumar Bhaduri's simple, realistic presentation of the character he portrayed, with a suitably appropriate air of modernity. The importance of suggestion was also made apparent in this performance. The dramatic critic of *Nautchghar* (27th Jaistha 1934 BS) remarks of Sisir Kumar Bhaduri's performance as in the works of the French poet Varlaine 'always suggestion, never statement, always a renunciation'. He also remarked that what Arthur Simon had said of Duse – 'And it conquers almost the last obstacle, as it turns the one wholly external art, based upon mere imitation, existing upon the commonest terms of illusion, triumphing by exaggeration into an art wholly subtle, and almost spiritual a suggestion, an evasion, a secrecy' could well be applied to Sisir Kumar Bhaduri.

In short, Sisir Kumar Bhaduri's rendering of the role was outstanding, his acting being of the very highest order, and positively he entranced his audiences.

An item published in *Nautchghar* (6th Sravan 1334 BS) will surely illustrate the enormous success of Sisir Kumar Bhaduri's performance. The editor remarked that he had received so many letters in praise of Sisir Kumar Bhaduri that even a succession of editions of his paper would not be able to feature every one of them. He therefore asked the pardon of numerous letter writers for the omission of their letters, though a good many were well worth publishing.

On the occasion of a Girish Chandra Memorial Day (1335 BS), Sisir Kumar Bhaduri staged *Prajulla* at his own theatre. On this occasion it was Girish Chandra's son Dani Babu who took the part of Jogesh while Sisir Kumar Bhaduri played the role of Ramesh. It was for the first time that he appeared in this role. Sailen Chowdhury took the part of Suresh and Kartick Babu that of Pitambar. Another renowned actor Nirmalendu Lahiri took the part of Bhajahari. The actresses Tarasundari, Prova, Kusumkumari, Sushilabala and Ascharyamoyee portrayed respectively the roles of Umasundari, Prafulla, Jnanoda, Jagamoni and Matalini. Chittaranjan Goswami, Monoranjan Bhattacharya, Krishna Chandra De and others also took part in this performance. It was a distinguished performance indeed, both the acting and singing being outstanding and it is hardly surprising that all tickets were sold well in advance.

The article would indeed be incomplete without a reference to Sisir Kumar Bhaduri's performances in some of the tragic and heartrending plays of Girish Chandra such as *Balidan*. In his portrayal of the role of Karumay in *Balidan* Sisir Kumar Bhaduri's performance often caused members of the audience to break down, sob, and not just have tears gather in their eyes. Sisir Kumar Bhaduri also appeared in the role of Dulalchand in the play *Balidan*.

Audiences were also once privileged to see Sisir Kumar Bhaduri in the title role of *Bilwamangal*. It was the first time he had taken part in a play with a religious theme. So effectively did he play the role as to demonstrate beyond doubt that for a gifted actor it was not only possible but easy to assume any character.

Apart from the performances mentioned above, Sisir Kumar Bhaduri played different roles on the professional stage in plays of Girish Chandra such as *Ashoke*, *Pandav Gourav* etc. His genius would make most vivid each character he portrayed. These performances are recorded for all time in the history of the Bengali stage. It may also be mentioned here that the very last performance staged at Sisir Kumar Bhaduri's theatre *Sree Rangam* before it closed down was Girish Chandra's *Prafulla*.

Long before Independence Sisir Kumar Bhaduri had consistently done his best to have the ban withdrawn from Girish Chandra's patriot plays which the British Government had imposed. Each year at Girish Chandra memorial celebrations he would make his theatre available for the organizers without any charge and would join the meeting to pay homage to Girish Chandra and request the senior Government official who would come to preside to exert themselves to have the ban withdrawn from Girish Chandra's patriotic plays. His efforts were crowned with success after Independence. The ban on *Sirajudaulla* was lifted and Sisir Kumar Bhaduri arranged to stage a performance of this. He confined himself to the direction for the first few nights but later played the part of Siraj himself.

Although Sisir Kumar Bhaduri had only met Girish Chandra twice he had had the good fortune to see him on the stage a number of times. He had the very highest opinion of Girish Chandra as an actor and was enthusiastic about his manly appearances and grave but melodious voice.

On one occasion, distinguished audience including Sir Lewis Casson and Dame Sybil Throndike came to see Sisir Kumar Bhaduri in a performance of Michael Madhusudan. At the conclusion of the play, in reply to their spontaneous and sincere congratulations, he remarked that it was a pity that they had not seen a Bengali actor of the calibre of Girish Chandra.

When the admirers of Girish Chandra were trying to arrange for a marble statue of his to be set up at Girish Park, Sisir Kumar Bhaduri lent them every assistance. He arranged to have a benefit performance at his own theatre. *Prafulla*, the play that always remains fresh, was staged, and the entire proceeds were made over to those who had undertaken the responsibility of having a marble statue of Girish Chandra set up.

The article may fittingly conclude with a remark Sisir Kumar Bhaduri once made to the writer in the course of a discussion on Girish Chandra. He said, 'I can raise my hat off only to Girish Chandra and nobody else'.

First published as *'Sisir Bhaduri in Girish Chandra's Plays'*,
The Sunday Hindustan Standard: 14.08.1966

ANNEXURE - 1

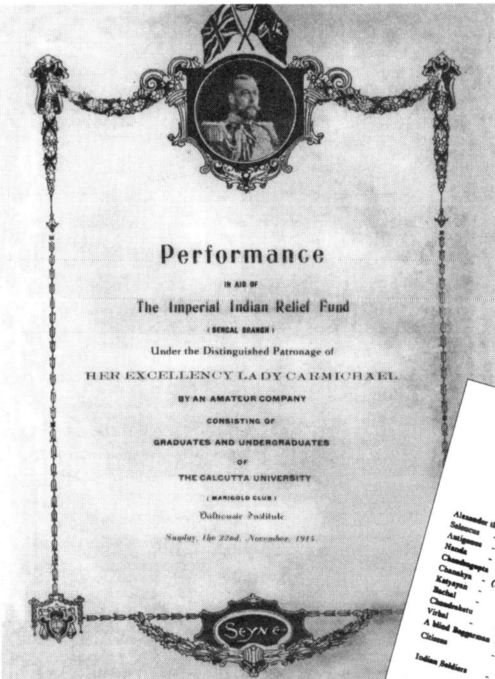

Performance

IN AID OF

The Imperial Indian Relief Fund

(BENGAL BRANCH)

Under the Distinguished Patronage of

HER EXCELLENCY LADY CARMICHAEL

BY AN AMATEUR COMPANY

CONSISTING OF

GRADUATES AND UNDERGRADUATES

OF

THE CALCUTTA UNIVERSITY

(MARIGOLD CLUB)

Dalhousie Institute

Sunday, the 22nd. November, 1915.

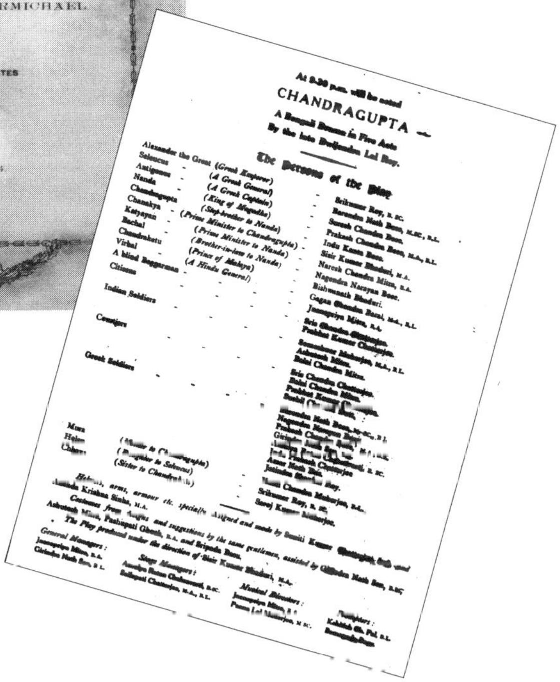

At 9-30 p.m. will be acted

CHANDRAGUPTA —

A Bengali Drama in Five Acts

By the late Dwijendra Lal Roy.

The Persons of the Play

Alexander the Great (Greek Emperor) - Srikumar Roy, B.Sc.

Seleucus - (A Greek General) - Barendra Nath Bose, M.Sc., B.L.

Antigonus - (A Greek Captain) - Suresh Chandra Bose.

Nanda - (King of Magadha) - Prakash Chandra Bose, M.A., B.L.

Chandragupta (Step-brother to Nanda) - Indu Kanta Bose.

Chanakya - (Prime Minister to Nanda) - Sisir Kumar Bhaduri, M.A.

Katyayan - (Prime Minister to Chandragupta) - Naresh Chandra Mitra, B.A.

Bachal - (Brother-in-law to Nanda) - Nagendra Narayan Bose.

Chandraketu (Prince of Malaya) - Bishwanath Bhaduri.

Virbal - (A Hindu General) - Gagan Chandra Basu, M.A., B.L.

A blind Beggarman - [illegible]

Citizens - [illegible]

Indian Soldiers - [illegible]

Courtiers - [illegible]

Greek Soldiers - [illegible]

Mura - [illegible]

Helen (Daughter to Seleucus) - [illegible]

Chhaya (Sister to Chandraketu) - [illegible]

Helmets, arms, armour etc. specially designed and made by [illegible]

Costumes from [illegible] and suggestions by the same gentlemen, assisted by [illegible]

The Play produced under the direction of Sisir Kumar Bhaduri, M.A.

General Managers: [illegible]

Stage Managers: [illegible]

Musical Directors: [illegible]

Prompters: [illegible]

At 9.30 p.m. will be acted

CHANDRAGUPTA

A Bengali Drama in five Acts
By the late Dwijendra Lal Roy.

The persons of the play

Alexander the Great	*(Greek Emperor)*	–	Srikumar Roy, B.SC.
Seleucus	*(A Greek General)*	–	Barendra Nath Bose, M.SC, B.L.
Antigonus	*(A Greek Captain)*	–	Suresh Chandra Bose,
Nanda	*(King of Magadha)*	–	Prakash Chandra Bose, M.A., B.L.
Chandragupta	*(Step-Brother to Nanda)*	–	Indu Kanta Bose.
Chanakya	*(Prime Minister to Chandragupta)*	–	Sisir Kumar Bhaduri, M.A.
Katyayan	*(Prime Minister to Nanda)*	–	Naresh Chandra Mitra, B.A.
Bachal	*(Brother-in-law to Nanda)*	–	Nagendra Narayan Bose.
Chandraketu	*(Prince of Malaya)*	–	Bishwanath Bhaduri.
Virbal	*(A Hindu General)*	–	Gagan Chandra Baral, M.A., B.L.
A blind Beggarman		–	Jnanpriya Mitra, B.A.
Citizens		–	Sris Chandra Chatterjee. Prabhat Kumar Chatterjee
Indian Soldiers		–	Someshwar Mukerjee, M.A., B.L. Ashutosh Mitra. Balai Chandra Mitra.
Courtiers		–	Sris Chandra Chatterjee. Balai Chandra Mitra. Prabhat Kumar Chatterjee. Sushil Chandra Dutt.
Greek Soldiers		–	Barendra Nath Bose, M.SC, B.L. Nagendra Narayan Bose. Prakash Chandra Bose, M.A., B.L. Girindra Nath Sen, B. L. Amulya Ratan Chakravarti, B. SC. Indu Prakash Chatterjee. Amar nath Das. Jatindra Shankar Roy.
Mura	*(Mother to Chandragupta)*	–	Kanti Chandr Mukerjee, B. L.
Helen	*(Daughter to Seleucus)*	–	Srikumar Roy, B. SC
Chhaya	*(Sister to Chandraketu)*	–	Saroj Kumar Mukerjee.

Helmets, arms, armour etc. specially designed and made by Suniti Kumar Chatterjee, M.A. *and* Ananda Krishna Sinha, M.A.

Costumes from designs and suggestions by the same gentlemen, assisted by Girindra Nath Sen, B.L., Ashutosh Mitra, Pashupati Ghosh, B.A. *and* Sripada Basu.

The play produced under the direction of Sisir Kumar Bhaduri, M.A.

General Managers:	Stage Managers:	Musical Directors:	Prompters:
Jananpriya Mitra B.A.	Amulya Ratan Chakravarti B.SC.	Jnanapriya Mitra B.A.	Kshitsh Ch. Pal B.A.
Cirindra Nath Sen B.L.	Sailapati Chatterjee M.A., B.L.	Panna Lal Mukerjee M.SC.	Bamapada Basu

SYNOPSIS

Chandragupta was a half-brother to Nanda, king of Magadha.

Nanda hated Chandragupta and his mother Mura because the latter was of humble birth. Chandragupta was forced for some time to live as an exile with the Greeks under Alexander the Great. He made friends with Chandraketu, Prince of Malya, and Chandraketu's sister Chhaya loved him. With the assistance of his friend with the advice and guidance of the astute Chanakya, who had pledged himself to overthrow Nanda as the latter had once insulted him, Chandragupta defeated Nanda and became king of Magadha.

Once in power, he forgot the services of Chanakya, of whom he became jealous, and treated Chandraketu as his vassal. Trying to assert himself he offended Chankya, who gave up his charge just at the time when the new king's position was threatened by internal revolts and by internal revolts and by attacks from without by the Greeks under Seleucus. Through the importunacy of Mura and Chandraketu, Chanakya was induced to come to the rescue once more. The Plots were suppressed and the rebels punished, and Seleucus was defeated and captured with his daughter Helen.

Peace was concluded with the Greek king, who ceded some territories and whose daughter, according to the terms of the treaty, was to marry Chandragupta. Mura, on the other hand, touched by the sweetness of Chhaya and her enthusiasm for Chandragupta's cause, had resolved to make her her son's bride. The arrangement by which Chandragupta was to marry Helen gave Chhaya great shock, but she resolved to suffer silently if by that marriage all would be well. She came to see the royal pair, and an unexpected *dénouement* took place when Helen asked Chhaya to be a sister to her, so that they might be 'two sister-streams, merging into the same ocean,' and made her place the bridal necklace on Chandragupta.

The great historical events upon which the play is based took place about B. C. 320.

The author of the play, the late Dwijendra Lal Roy, who died in May last year, was during his lifetime one of the forces in the domain of

Bengali Literature. He was an alumnus of the royal Agricultural College at Cirencester, and a member of the Bengal Civil Services. He wrote a large number of historical dramas which are widely popular. But his best gift to his nation is his songs. He gave to Bengal a new *genre,* the comic song, and it is unanimously held by his countrymen that his name will live mainly through his songs.

"Chandragupta" – a leaflet of play produced by students of Calcutta University ('Marigold Club') on 22nd November, 1914

ANNEXURE - 2

A National Theatre for Calcutta

By Natyacharya Sisir Kumar Bhaduri

Declining the honour of 'Padmabhusan' Natyacharya Sisir Kumar Bhaduri wrote to the Government of India that a fitter honour bestowed upon him, and, through himself, the cause to which he had given the best years of his life, would have been the gift of a public stage to the city of Calcutta.

Below Natyacharya Bhaduri explains in this article specially written for the readers of Hindusthan Standard *what he has in view when he speaks of a National Theatre.*

Why, I have been asked, do I ask for a National Theatre?

The answer is very simple. Calcutta is the only city in India in which there has been for the last eighty years several professional Theatre houses which cater to a large number of pople who thirst for entertainment of a higher order – which pleases not merely their senses but also appeals to their intellect.

The professional theatre in Bengal began nearly ninety years ago. It had from the very beginning a strong commercial bias. But a succession of great actor-managers did not allow Bengali theatre to degenerate into Grand Guignol, though there was always a tendency to do so. During the last ten years, however, Bengali theatre has suffered considerably from the impact of the cinema, both financially and from the artistic stand-point. Mostly plays are put on stage which owe their inspiration to the cinema. Great old plays are very rarely revived.

ESSENTIAL FUNCTIONS

I would say that one of the essential functions of the national theatre would be to hold up before Bengali audiences the vista of Bengal's past as expressed in the dramas which have powerfully stirred the Bengali mind and shaped it.

At the same time, all of us realise that our own times, and some of our hopes, must be expressed to our people through the stage. A mere repetition of the old plays will not be enough for this.

Some of the reformers of our times imagine that the method by which such modern plays should be written and put over is by re-writing, say, the Five-Year Plan, in a play form. One grave danger of a State-owned theatre is just here that the State would always be anxious to use the powerful medium of the stage for putting over their "handouts".

A play is a play. People come to it to be entertained. When it fails to entertain, it becomes not a play but just a sermon, a propaganda medium. A good play is one where people come to be entertained, are entertained, and yet go away with some impression in their minds which touches the core of their being. All good art creates this impression. Art has to be defined and created in terms of art; we cannot create art in an inartistic mould, however good its content.

It is not easy to write a play. The discipline of the stage must enter into it through all its nuances. It is therefore necessary for a playwright and a producer to work together. The playwright insists upon a new kind of play, the producer has to try it out on the stage and find out how far it is possible to do it in the most impressive manner.

In the writing of new plays and in the manner of producing them, a great deal of experimentation is necessary before successful new plays or new modes can be realized.

Amateur and semi-professional organisations are trying out such experimentation with some success. Bengali drama is still full of promise. But the noticeable feature in this field of activity is that they are small-scale. A great drama is not being produced to-day in the big theatres. Why is this so?

STANDARDISED PLAYS

The answer is not far to seek. The capitalists who own Theatre houses are afraid of running risks. They are afraid of experimentation. They believe in standardised plays and a standardised manner of acting. They have no faith in freshness either in methods of acting or in the production of plays.

The result is that experimentation is restricted, and we have on the professional stage monotonous and meaningless repetition of the same type of plays, and often the same play.

The commercial theatres do spend a lot of money on their production. The lack is not of money but of orientation. Hackneyed manners of production, dramatisation of popular novels, even of successful films, pass current on our professional stage.

It is necessary to relieve Bengali drama from this cramp which has seized it.

GOOD PLAYS

I do not for one moment suggest that a new Five or Three-Act Play, which has a great inspiration at its source, cannot or will not fetch money from the audience.

Speaking as a producer-actor, I say that it was very rarely the audience which let me down. I have throughout my dramatic career believed in putting over plays which I considered worthwhile. The audience have nearly always thronged to see them. But the difference between a purely commercial outlook and the outlook which should inspire a National Theatre is that while the main object of a commercial theatre is to make money, whether it produces a good play or not, the National Theatre should produce only good plays, whether every such play fetches money or not. The inspiration should be not earning money, but to serve nationalism in the field of drama. Properly managed, there is no reason why it should get into heavy deficits. For, I have just said, our people like good plays.

But the National Theatre must not hope to depend for its existence on the booking office. It must have an adequate endowment to help

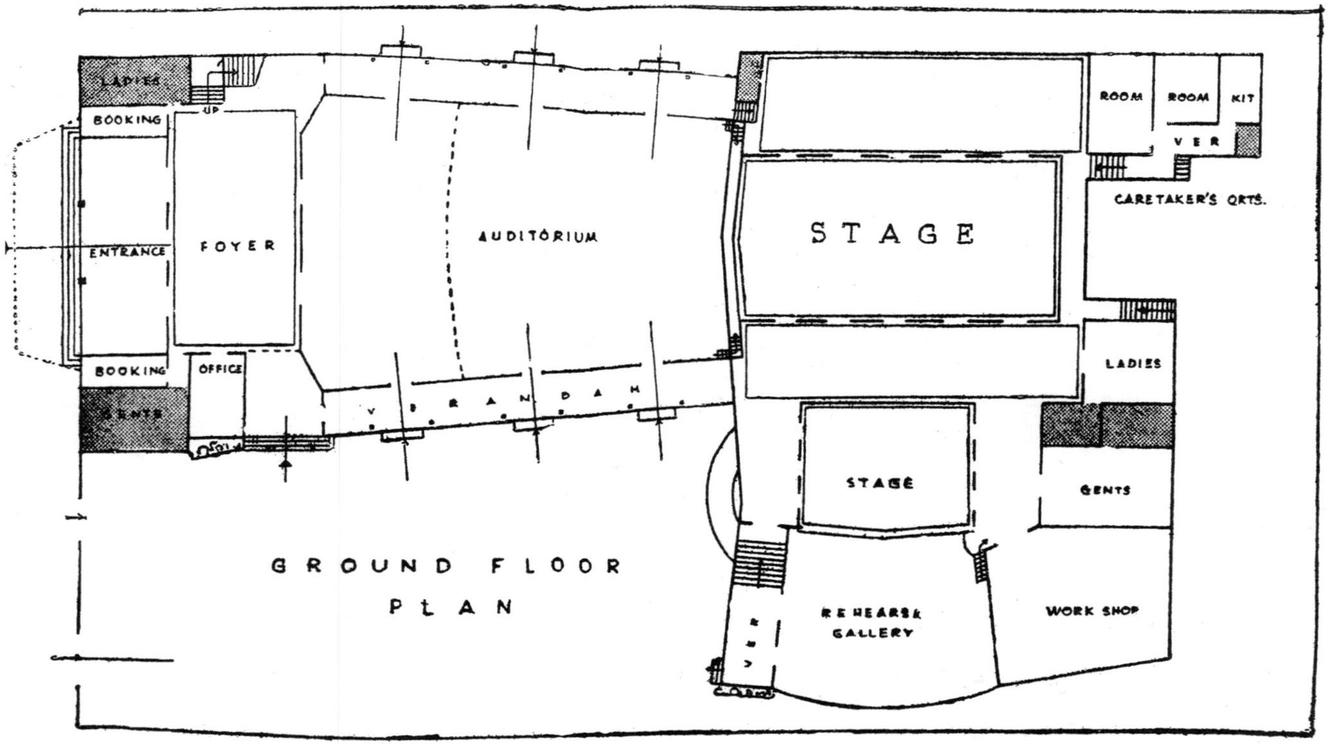

PROPOSED PEOPLE'S THEATRE AT CALCUTTA
Ground Floor Accommodation : 750. First Floor Accommodation : 250.
Approximate Plinth Area : 17,500 Sq. Feet., Approximate Cost Rs. 6,50,000

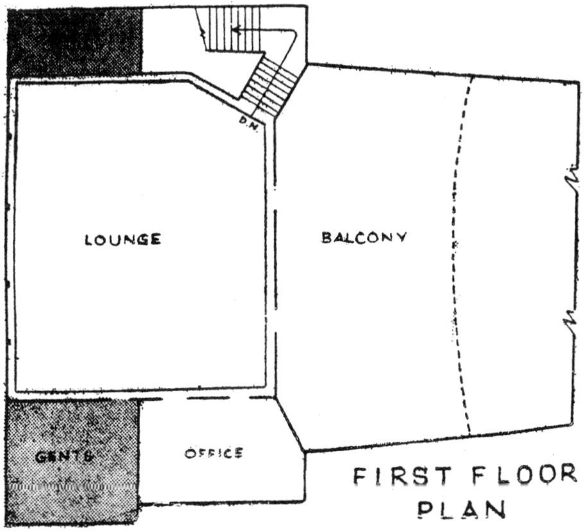

FIRST FLOOR PLAN

it over lean seasons, and sufficient capital for a start. The National Theatre is really to be the name for an endowed Theatre which can fearlessly experiment; where people may have continued opportunity for seeing the best drama, best and forecast past and pre-indigenous, or adaptation translation from our and foreign classics. These should be produced with utmost distinction, and play by *a permanent company of the highest merit.*

Who should own theatre?

A NATIONAL PROPERTY

When it is built, equipped and endowed, the Theatre will be presented to the nation and will be administered by a body of public trustees with a Director who will have control of the artistic side, the management. The management of the theatre should efficient. It should not fall in the hands of the set group; it should serve national and not sectional ends.

First published as *'A National Theatre for Calcutta by Natyacharya Sisir Kumar Bhaduri'* in *The Sunday Hindustan Standard*, Calcutta, 22nd March, 1959